CONSTRUCTION
BUSINESS

I0396561

PREM
VARDHAN

INDIA · SINGAPORE · MALAYSIA

Notion Press

Old No. 38, New No. 6
McNichols Road, Chetpet
Chennai - 600 031

First Published by Notion Press 2020
Copyright © Prem Vardhan 2020
All Rights Reserved.

ISBN 978-1-64783-626-9

Contents

Preface

I have tried to explain, systems, procedures, precautions and general basic concepts of contracting from the time one thinks of becoming a contractor and have undertaken this journey to explain most of major aspects of contracting for mega projects.

I have elaborated further on understanding business in different streams of contracting. The entrepreneur should select a stream of his choice and opportunity, concentrate on that stream first instead of working on different streams right from beginning. However, I have come across a new and different challenge on every project in my career. I could succeed since I was an employee and a big organization was always up to support me in cases of difficulties, changes in methods of construction and resource requirements. I was always learning while working.

This work provides almost complete insight on methods of construction, quality parameters, project management, planning, costing, tendering and billing.

Right from basic earthwork to building high embankments, rock blasting—both, open cast and underwater—roads, various types of concreting including, RCC, pre-stressed concrete, underwater and roller-compacted concrete, slip form structures, steel structures fabrication and erection and many more methods of building projects and their applications in this industry for mega construction projects.

As emphasized in this book, my advice is that slow and steady wins the race.

I am always available for any advice/guidance.

Best wishes,

– Prem Vardhan

vardhanprem@yahoo.com
+91 9769739826 (Mumbai)

Acknowledgement

This work is dedicated to my teacher SRI SHASHI RUIA, Chairman, ESSAR Group of Companies

Respectful regards

– Prem Vardhan

01

Introduction

Many young men with innovative capabilities and risk-taking abilities search for construction business opportunities since it is one which can be started easily, and with least investment.

Success depends on various factors like implementation of innovative ideas, interest in solving problems, guidance from experienced personnel and continued business opportunities. However, some uncertainty may prevail in initial jobs, just like in any other business.

This business can be started with a small capital, it is affordable and in case of setbacks, there should be no regrets. The bigger the investment, the bigger the risk and the bigger the size of first jobs—it all depends upon the opportunities and the appetite of the entrepreneur.

Some people in desperate search of some work often approach project engineers for assignments and—no wonder—one day become respectable contractors. They get about 15% for supervision and profit on actual wages paid to workers; they start with 15 to 20 workers and slowly grow. If the project manager is kind enough, the business gets paid early and pays workers after getting paid by main contractor.

After completing an assignment successfully, if continuous work is not available, one tends to lose heavily due to idling of resources. Hence, newly-purchased resource mobilization in initial jobs should be minimal and hired resources should be utilized as far as possible, who can be released without any additional costs.

It is very common in construction businesses for last bills to get delayed due to some reason or other. The contractor must somehow pay his creditors without waiting for payment of the last bill from client. Hence,

- Efforts should always be made to recover maximum possible money from client before finishing the job.

- In cases of uncertainty of getting money from client, sufficient funds should be kept in reserve to clear creditor's payments.

Due to idling of resources and other such constraints, the contractor starts searching for a new job desperately and makes bigger mistakes by quoting low prices or accepting difficult jobs. Such approaches often complicate issues further, making it difficult to come out of problems. **Hence, construction businesses should always be started in a small way so as to have no regrets if there is not much scope of success in initial contracts. There should not be any desperation, hurry or undue excitements which could result in big mistakes.**

Further, he should avoid making heavy investments in the beginning under any circumstances. There will be many more opportunities to make such investments in the future. He must keep some cash reserve for rainy days. One should have the capacity to take care of his personal requirements from other resources for about two years. Profits should not be eaten away in the beginning itself and there must be no regrets if the first set of investments in this new business are lost.

It would be ideal if 50% profits are rolled back into the business and the rest are kept in deposits needed for providing securities and other unforeseen expenses.

Even well-experienced engineers start contracting businesses for themselves in a small way only. Mostly, successful engineers are not necessarily successful contractors when they **start contracting with their own money.**

They do not have the means to turn out the same volumes of business as while in employment with big contractors and, therefore are not able to fully compromise with their status and keep spending on themselves and overheads which are not affordable for his small business.

The most important thing is keeping expenses within the budget. A person earning 500,000 per month as salary while in employment would like to earn at least 300,000+ for contingencies, to remain afloat in business. If you wish to earn 500,000 per month in the initial stages of the business, it will need an investment of at least 50 million. This is simple calculation. Banks give you hardly 0.5% per month on deposits while we are talking 1% returns on investment per month in the initial period; is it not optimistic? That too is very difficult. Once you know the trade and start making real money, it will be your money and you can spend it the way you like. Further, you cannot spend for all the investments in the first month itself and start earning reasonably.

It is not a gamble since success depends on your careful selection of jobs, execution team, efforts in the right direction and support from the client. Just riding a bicycle is easy but initially, it is difficult; one needs support.

1.1 Contracting business is much safer than opening a shop.

Alternatively, even if one opens a small shop, there would be fixed costs such as rentals, regular maintenance and minimum stock to be maintained.

Selection of items and their quantities for initial stock is always a challenge. Stock-levels should be such that one can service the first a few customers, fulfilling all their requirements at competitive prices. For continued business, these customers should come back to your shop for further purchases and get introduced to others. Stocks should be replenished as per sales and market requirements.

Many shops close after some time with losses due to something or the other lagging and not being able to recover even the maintenance costs. Even the location of the shop and selection of items to be sold are important factors for success.

If you go to a chemist's shop, asked for some rarely-sold medicines and all were available, it would create a good impression and you would like to go there again and again. Further, if inadvertently you order on phone just one strip of a cheap medicine late in the evening and this man at your doorstep with the medicine in no time, you would become his regular customer. This is good marketing. But, one should have knowledge/guidance on what all should be included in the first fill of stocks.

1.2 Diversification in new businesses

Once the construction business is well-established and surplus cash is available, say after a minimum of ten years, the entrepreneur should start some manufacturing or other related business side-by-side for stability and expansion of business in different streams.

Generally, contractor's children do not feel comfortable in going through the grind their parents have gone through, without which it is difficult to prosper in construction businesses. Hence, some alternatives have to be thought of for the next generation, unless children have similar interests and commitment to continue the construction business.

1.3 Some smart children often make the mistake of thinking they will employ good professionals to manage the business.

The performance of many professionally-managed construction companies in the world remains good due to skills and interests of a few senior executives.

1. These executives are highly trustworthy and efficient, with powers and emoluments like owners, with very high incentives/dividends being offered upon success. Still, the owner has to be continuously vigilant and involved.

2. Any change of management has a good or bad effect on the performance of the company.

3. These construction companies are mostly not even close to the richest business houses in the society unless they diversify in other businesses.

In 1979, a professionally-managed company in Oman had liquidated damages accumulated on a single project of the Petroleum Development of Oman in Fahud oil fields—the amount was more than the net worth of the company! They changed just three executives in top management to come out of the threat of closure of the company. In less than one year, they started making profits on many new jobs.

In 1967, a young contractor was taking small but challenging contracts at comfortable prices. Within forty years, he became one of the biggest industrialists of India. Effectively, he was the project manager for all of his business establishments—the key reason for his success.

John C Gammon, after a First-Class Honours in Engineering from London joined the Public Works Department of India as Assistant Engineer in 1910. In 1919, as a small contractor, he built the foundation to the prestigious Gateway of India. Three years later, in 1922, he established J.C. Gammon Ltd. He continued to expand his horizon across the Commonwealth, Asia and West Africa. Though their activities spread far and wide, Gammon India continued to be the root source where Sir. J.C. Gammon first sowed the seed of his remarkable vision, growing into one of landmarks of our construction industry.

We will be deliberating this journey in detail in this book, with success stories and practical tips to help one become a successful contractor in their life. We will start with small jobs and slowly graduate to international, mega construction projects, including their planning and costing with dos and don'ts.

02

Start of a Construction Business

As stated earlier, construction businesses can even be started in a small way with the investment of one's own time and money for salary of a few staff/workers for a few months. It could even be initially operated from home.

There should not be any capital investment or high overheads till the first job is awarded. Even then, investments should be slow and as per actual, urgent requirement, progress of work on the project and cash inflow. Any hurry, overconfidence or desperation due to time running out, etc. does not help. Invest in resources only when truly required. Too much delay in resource mobilization is also harmful. You could even hire resources from other agencies, for some time—till you are confident of assured of returns on investment.

It is not advisable to carry high inventory of assets at the end of a job, without cash in hand. Hence, unless totally paid off in the first contract or firm commitment of continuous business plus reasonable surplus cash is generated, equipment should be hired and not purchased.

A well-established, excellent-grade contractor executed his first highly-specialized construction contract in Mumbai with:

- His office-cum-residence in a most prestigious hotel.

- All his regular staff residences in good hotels with or without families.

- All vehicles and equipment hired on rental.

- Most of construction equipment on rentals except those which could be transferred from other jobs without any difficulty with least mobilization costs.

With this, it is very clearly understood that if he does not get the next job concurrent to finishing this job, he would have no idle assets to maintain and other liabilities in the expensive city. Further, **all profits were in cash**.

He had roaring business in and around Mumbai with many new contracts.

Eventually, after a decade, he even shifted his headquarters to Mumbai. This means no hasty decisions should be made on such important issues. He waited for more than a decade to make the decision to shift his headquarters.

2.1 A construction business can be started in either one of the following activities

- Procurement support for building materials

- Getting some work done on a project site by employing unskilled and semi-skilled workers as a labour contractor.

- Getting odd jobs done on unit-rate contracts including materials and skeleton construction equipment.

- Supplying construction equipment on rental including transport vehicles on long lease or taking equipment operation contracts on unit rates.

- Etc.

2.2 Procurement support

At one point in time, there was boom in the construction industry. A young boy took interest in the cement supply business. His father had a small cement shop. Hence, he knew a little about it. Cement is a perishable item, and therefore production and storage should be according to weekly/ monthly consumption. There were many factories in the vicinity and all were producing at 60 to 70% of their rated capacity. He went to a production unit and offered to sell part of their surplus capacity without approaching their current customers and negotiated a good commission since he would be marketing their surplus capacity of cement production. He approached a few major contractors and offered to provide cement procurement support at a price always lesser than the market price. He shared his hefty commission from the manufacturer with the contractors and made small but reasonable money in big volumes. At one point, he became one of the biggest cement sales organizers of the country.

For a construction company in the South Pacific, in a very remote area, a young man from Australia offered to provide procurement facilities at a commission of 2%. He would buy all the material to be imported for the project from Australia and New Zealand at competitive prices and arrange shipping. The arrangement worked very well for more than a year but soon, he became dishonest and started overcharging. Naturally, he was soon exposed and lost his roaring business.

Such arrangements are very common for projects in remote areas, needing material from distant market places. Commission agents and young entrepreneurs approach contractors soon after their getting the contract to provide them procurement management support.

2.3 Getting done some work on a project site by employing unskilled and semi-skilled workers as a labour contractor

Most of major contractors give away some easy and highly labour-intensive jobs to smaller agencies due to the following reasons:

- Their own cost of labour is high due to compliance of labour laws and other company policies.

- Overheads for time-keeping and management get reduced by giving sub-contract.

- Camp facilities including insurance, camp maintenance and other related costs are saved.

- Gratuity and termination benefits including threat of union-like atmosphere are avoided.

- Better output and save idling costs due to direct supervision.

- Etc.

If contractor gives highly labour-intensive and low-tech jobs to smaller contractors, he saves himself the headache of all the above management issues and saves his time and attention for better and more complicated issues, without loss of money. Small contractors usually work at a cost even lesser than the cost of these works so as to project and make profits. A small contractor makes profits by costs savings as under:

- He takes local and cheap unemployed workers or brings workers from nearby places. Technical training centres are also a source of getting skilled labour.

- Makeshift camps instead of a regular colony.

- Direct supervision; hence, better productivity with least overheads.

- All temporary appointments on casual basis for small periods. Hence, no gratuity, termination benefits, union, etc.

- Often, they don't even pay minimum wages.

- He lives and eats with the labourers in the same camp, in a separate and better accommodation nearby.

In addition, the main contractor provides some supervision and training to maintain quality of work for which, ultimately, he himself is responsible. This is a good learning process for a contractor.

With time, his interest and personal involvement, he learns the trade and starts delivering quality jobs with good productivity. The main contractor reduces his supervision and gives more, bigger jobs to the small contractor.

2.4 Getting odd jobs done on unit-rate contracts, including materials and skeleton construction equipment.

As contractor progresses slowly, he starts taking small contracts from the same or similar main contractors with his own materials like timber formwork, scaffolding material, stone chips, sand, paints for painting the buildings, electrical cables, conduits and switches as per specifications with construction equipment like a small truck, an excavator, small power generator for construction assistance, etc., and rapidly grows further.

2.5 No wonder—one day—a small contractor becomes a big contractor.

The size and duration of the first few jobs would depend upon the opportunity available, one's own personal interest, committed resources and confidence.

If the contractor has courage and is willing to risk investing, he could even start with a fairly big subcontract from the main contractor.

One of the main contractors on a major seaport project needed a few heavy cranes and barges to complete his contract but was avoiding investment and looking to rent equipment from somewhere. Incidentally, one young boy, the son of a wealthy family, was seriously planning to do something of his own and looking for an opportunity. He used to come for a stroll to this port site and observed that work was practically at a standstill. He went into the details, had lengthy discussions with the contractor, took the help of two engineer friends and then decided to invest in the required heavy marine construction equipment and took a sub-contract at comfortable rates.

The father of this young man arranged for bank finances with an assurance that he will earn and return the money to the bank. This was a wise step taken by the father. He could have given him all the money but now, the son would understand the value of money and be responsible for returning the money to the bank at the earliest, with interest.

One of these two engineers—a civil engineer—became the project manager and the other one, an expert in maintenance and operations of cranes, etc., became the operations in-charge.

This young man, the owner, personally stood at the site for long hours daily, supervising the job under the guidance of his friendly employees, finished the job before time and made good money. To his luck, he got another job needing the same equipment concurrent to finishing that project and then, there was no looking back.

These two friends were taken as employees at reasonable salaries of their choice and no profit sharing. This is always important for long-term association. If one is neither investing money nor sharing losses, he should not be a partner. He can be given hefty bonuses in proportion to the profits.

This works both ways—in the best interest of the employer and the employee. Profit is notional and making or not making profit on a job depends on many factors that could be managed or may create disputes.

Similarly, a young construction company on a large dam project—much bigger than their management capability—as part of employment conditions, agreed to pay a large sum as bonus to their project manager upon successful project completion. This project manager was selected after lots of scrutiny.

After successfully doing two jobs lasting more than six years, a way was found for the respectable exit of this project manager, since his skills were no more required and the contractor could manage on his own.

With success on the first few jobs, there will be confidence to take on bigger challenges. Many such entrepreneurs grow to become a big contractors and industrialists, with the care of not becoming over-enthusiastic at any time.

As one grows, his risks and responsibilities also become larger and larger with gaining expertise in many fields of the construction industry.

A young contractor started by buying stone chips from a quarry head, transported them with hired trucks and supplied to the main contractor. Slowly, he took the quarry on lease, purchased a few trucks and grew to the sky being the limit as a stone chips supplier in Uttar Pradesh.

2.6 Supplying construction equipment on rental, including transport vehicles on long lease or taking equipment operation contracts on unit rates.

Transport contracts are a big business all over the world. But to start, it needs a reference and a job order. If someone is willing to give a job order to transport some material between two locations regularly, he should be satisfied that you have requisite resources for the same. You need to explain to him to his satisfaction that you are seriously interested to do the business and are resourceful enough to procure/arrange for the necessary equipment. But, however, you would definitely be expecting a commitment for continued business for a reasonable time with compensations for idling of equipment when it is not your fault.

All major construction projects need sand, stone chips, timber and other products to be bought and brought from reasonably-long distances. Main contractors prefer to manage transport work within the project area and around with their equipment but often find it cheaper to give away transport work from long distances to others due to the following reasons:

Once the truck leaves the site, it is all in the control of the driver—his will, sincerity, efficiency and honesty, how he goes, loads the material and returns safely within the expected time.

- The driver could damage or pretend to have damaged the vehicle, causing delays and charging extra money on false repairs.

- He could steal fuel and lubricants.

- He could drive rashly, resulting more wear and tear, reduced life and efficiency of the vehicle.

- He could pick up passengers and extra loads on way for his benefits at the risk of overloading the vehicle.

- He could visit friends and relatives on way and waste time on duty.

- Sometimes, he could even indulge in smuggling of goods at the risk of the vehicle owner.

The person intending to enter this business has to satisfy first himself and then the main contractor about how he would take care of these issues and other related problems and not fail.

- This person should preferably be a driver himself.

- He should give almost 70% of the salary to the drivers as fixed pay and add reasonable expenses for above causes as an incentive per trip including cost of fuel to be paid by driver from this incentive allowance.

- He should not change drivers on the vehicles often unless there is a dire necessity. It is better if each truck is driven by one or two drivers only.

- Regular maintenance and change of tires when necessary for safe driving must be done.

- Even an offer can be made to give away the truck to the driver at a fixed discounted price after a certain number of kilometres are logged in and safely operating for 5 to 6 years.

His fleet should always remain young and efficient.

One can always find old cars, trucks and buses in depilated conditions doing light duty in town areas and vehicles running on long distances are in meticulous conditions.

2.7 Construction equipment like cranes, bulldozers and other heavy equipment renting.

Big cranes, excavators of different types, bulldozers and similar earthmoving equipment, barges, tugboats, launching equipment for bridges, and such expensive equipment are not advisable for a main contractor to keep and maintain in large numbers due to the paucity of continued business suitable for such specific equipment.

Contractors maintain a reasonable size of fleet of this equipment, without which it is even difficult to get jobs. Balance he takes from sub-contractors as per project's peak/initial requirements.

They rent such equipment to fill the gaps for peak demands and/or at the time of start of new contracts. If contractor's equipment is still busy on the job not finished, often start the project with rented equipment and release rented equipment after his own equipment arrive project site.

Agencies having such equipment are always in contact with many contractors and someone or the other always needs some equipment. Still, their yearly occupancy is around 70% to 80% after reasonably good marketing. Rental rates are calculated accordingly. Above 80% utilization is a bonus.

Taking contracts for equipment hiring.

If output is measurable, it is safe for the owner of the equipment as well as main contractor to work on unit rate of work done.

For general purpose equipment, it is generally a fixed amount of time—ten hours duty daily with weekly off. Any extra hours worked would be charged at hourly rate worked out by dividing the monthly rental rate by 250 hours a month.

For round-the-clock operations, the following arrangement could be considered:

Rates are fixed for a minimum of 15 hours a day's work, i.e., 370 to 400 hours a month.

A minimum number of working hours to be paid is part of the contract.

- Payments on the basis of actual working hours (minimum hours as per contract to be paid anyway) are calculated on a start-of-engine to stop-of-engine basis. The logbook is to be maintained and signed on a daily basis.

- Any extra hours worked would be paid on a pro-rata basis.

- Working hours – Two shifts of ten continuous hours each. The balance of four hours a day is for maintenance. It takes two hours for the engine to cool down and then two hours for topping up of fuel, lubricants, hydraulic oils, greasing of vital components and general check-ups.

- Accommodation, transport and food for crew to be arranged by equipment owner or as agreed.

- Salaries, wages, bonus, medical support, etc., for all the operators and crew to be paid by the equipment owner directly without involvement of hirer/main contractor. This should not go to the hands of the main contractor. Else, the owner will lose control.

- Insurance for workmen and equipment for total loss at replacement cost not depreciated book value) to be negotiated but beneficiary has to be the equipment owner.

- Mobilization and demobilization on main contractor's account.

- For heavy-duty cranes, the owner should provide new one-time lifting gear including wire ropes conforming to safety requirements. Any new replacements made during the contract to be made on the main contractor's account or as agreed.

- Automatic Siren on overloading to be installed on the equipment.

- Fuel, lubricants filters, etc., to be charged to owner's account. The main contractor could also provide fuel and lubricants on a chargeable basis.

2.8 Dry leasing

Dry leasing is a system by which the owner just provides his equipment on a fixed time-charter basis. Complete operation and maintenance is charged to the account of the main contractor as if he is the owner of the equipment.

The main contractor provides operators, fuel and all other costs including maintenance and repairs at his own cost.

A thorough survey is conducted before and after the contract period and handing over the equipment to each other by a certified surveyor. Any damages beyond normal wear and tear to be made good by the main contractor within lease agreement. He has to pay rentals for time spent on repairs.

Adequate insurance cover is taken by the owner of the equipment for the charter-hire period for the total loss of equipment.

This system is adopted for heavy marine construction/transport equipment. Sometimes, governments also provide their equipment, if available, on a dry-lease basis to their contractors on large projects.

Above all, all the conditions of the contract must be framed very carefully. An example of a minor but serious mistake by the owner of equipment is as follows:

Around 1965, the Indian government procured a big fleet of brand new earthmoving equipment for a major dam project in Uttar Pradesh on an Indo-American friendship program. At that time, America was providing construction equipment at highly discounted prices to India for selected mega projects.

The Indian government gave this equipment to the contractor on payment of carefully-calculated monthly **depreciation** costs, depreciating equipment to a near-zero value by the end of the project, thinking that they would recover full cost of equipment from the contractor and would still own the equipment at the end of the project, in whatever condition it may be.

At end of the project, the contractor managed to take all the equipment through court interventions for practically free, on the pretext that the equipment was in excellent condition at the end of the project due to good maintenance and upkeep by the contractor who had paid the cost of the equipment by paying the depreciation fixed by the government. Hence, only the residual value of the equipment, as per books of accounts, was paid by the contractor to the government after completing the job, which was negligible. The contract was also silent on the status of ownership of equipment at the end of the project.

He finished many projects with that equipment thereafter. **Writing in the contract, the word *depreciation* instead of *rental*, turned the table and the department lost the case in the court**.

In 2011, a smart, portable, tented residential and office accommodation supplier gave his tents for two years on monthly rental basis to a contractor for his project in a remote area on the basis of his recovering almost 90% of costs in two years, and in case of any extension of time, rentals to be paid were the same as monthly rates that were agreed upon. Somehow, the contractor could not return the tents for more than three years. The tent supplier, in the end, took more than one and a half times the cost of new tents from the contractor and still owned the tents in good condition.

At one time, there was very heavy customs duty in India on import of special equipment by private operators but the government had some concessions for their mega-projects. A contractor put a condition in his contract that the government would supply some specified equipment on rental basis for his use on the project. Rental for equipment was less than 70% of landed costs. With this condition, he saved a big investment and reduced contract price, to get the contract. He returned the equipment on an as-and-where basis after finishing the project. This equipment had no immediate use for the contractor after finishing of that job.

Costing for leased equipment should cover following costs at the minimum:

All costs that are given in percentages are of landed cost of equipment per year.

Depreciation	12%
Repairs and maintenance	15%
Interest on investment	2.5%
Insurance	1.5%
Operations and fuel expenses	15%
Taxes and duties excluding income tax	4%
Contingencies	5%
Profit	15%

Total price for wet leasing for a contract per year = 70% of cost of equipment.

However, these numbers drastically change for different types of equipment and the above-stated numbers are just illustrations.

In such cases, yearly depreciation is charged on residual value of the equipment at the end of each year.

If the cost of new equipment is 100, its residual value after one year would be reduced to 88 and depreciation charged would be 12% of 88 = 10.56% of the cost of new equipment and so on while, repairs costs increase in similar magnitudes.

Initially, it looks like the maintenance cost is negligible but the first dry-docking/major overhaul is very expensive. Savings in maintenance costs should be kept in a separate account for spending on such overhauls.

As the equipment becomes older, its depreciation costs keep reducing and simultaneously repairs and maintenance costs increase. The sum of these two costs varies by 25% to 30% of replacement cost of equipment, while the residual cost may be practically nothing.

Efficiency of the equipment also reduces with age.

All government and other statutory bodies allow re-evaluation of equipment periodically and adjust their values in books of accounts and other documents.

Depending on upkeep, maintenance and usage, a decision is made about when to stop using the equipment for commercial purposes. Some entrepreneurs sell off equipment fast to keep their fleet young but such decisions should not be taken in a hurry to avoid regrets.

Based on above table, dry leasing could be 35 to 40% per year of the cost of the equipment. (Depreciation, interest, contingencies and profits)

Dry leasing of a Young fleet is a bit tricky and contracts should be worded very carefully.

Young fleet

Maintaining a Young fleet of equipment has many advantages:

- Maintenance cost is low

- Less overheads

- Productivity is good

- Better rental prices

- Lesser problems

- Status symbol

It is not advisable to new entrepreneurs to change their fleet quickly since real profit starts flowing in after equipment is fully paid off. There is very little difference in rentals of new equipment and slightly old equipment.

By the time the equipment is two to three years old, maintenance crew gets to know all about the equipment and will be able to handle even major problems.

If one goes to buy a premier car, the dealer offers a buy-back price after three to four years use and you could exchange it for a new model. This is not economics but a status requirement which is not advisable to new business houses. They should restrain from such luxuries till they are fully established.

Hospitals known for handling complex medical problems have an understanding with suppliers of equipment like MRI, CT scan, etc., to change the equipment upon availability of superior models. They replace equipment with newer models and take away two to three-year-old equipment to sell in the secondary market. This is important for such hospitals to keep in pace with the latest technology and developments.

Vendors providing similar services with grade lower equipment also charge less for a similar job. This also satisfies doctors dealing with less complicated cases.

Premier airlines keep their latest fleet of aircrafts only for a few prestigious sectors and downgraded aircrafts for less-important sectors. In the process, there is a planned and continuous upgradation of fleet, releasing aircrafts after their full utilization. There are three to four tiers of quality of aircrafts deployed in the same airline.

All transport contractors use the same system for phasing out old equipment like buses, cars, trucks, etc.

2.9 Second-hand equipment.

Purchase or wet lease of good second-hand equipment is a preferred proposition for new players.

Owners sell their equipment if either they are likely to be idle for long period or their maintenance cost becomes prohibitive. If an experienced contractor with all the facilities and knowledge of the problems of a particular equipment is reluctant to keep them, how can a new person in business, totally ignorant of defects in the equipment, be able to use it gainfully? Hence, old equipment should have at least one-year maintenance included in the sale contract and a major sum of money should be paid after successfully running the equipment for a certain period agreed upon in the contract.

On a major off-shore contract, a contractor needed four heavy-duty air compressors working round the clock and only one compressor could be stopped for refuelling and maintenance for four hours each in a day, in rotation. An equipment supplier brought five compressors in combination of new and old compressors, one being a stand-by option and deputed good, experienced crew and finished the job successfully.

Many subcontractors working on the project offered to buy old equipment from the contractor (contractor being the first owner) at discounted prices since they have seen operations and repairs of such particular equipment.

One of the top-level contractors of India was, way back, working with a French contractor on a mega-project as a small sub-contractor. At end of the project, the main contractor was not willing to continue in India due to paucity of immediate new contracts. This sub-contractor purchased all their sellable equipment at discounted prices and adjusted the prices against his outstanding.

With this equipment, he expanded his business many folds and there was no looking back.

The best alternative is lease of old equipment for one or two years and then purchase and all costs are to be agreed upon before start of the lease-cum-sales contract.

If one buys a second-hand car from a shop, the shopkeeper provides one-year warranty for performance of the car.

Equipment beyond economical repairs

Once equipment gets worn out and is beyond economical repairs and has served its full life, it is scraped and sold at a throw-away price to scrap dealers. These dealers take the equipment to designated yards for breaking down into small parts for repairs and disposal. All such yards have highly-skilled workers trained on the job. They are born, brought up trained while working and work there till the end, thus keeping their skills always alive by continuously improving them and passing them on through generations.

Many scrap dealers have their workshops in various parts of the country. They all deal only with one or two brands and types of equipment.

All scrap equipment of their interest is sent to their workshops.

- Here, the equipment is first dismantled in small parts.

- It is carefully cleaned of mud and rust and then examined.

- Usable items are repaired, including welding and machining.

- Distorted bearing housings are machined and if necessary, additional sleeves of similar metal are fixed.

- Even bearings are made in their makeshift workshops with good efficiency and performance.

- Electrical, electronics, hydraulic systems, engines, etc. are repaired or scrapped.

Now, they reassemble equipment with good and serviceable repaired parts and produce, say, four out of six equipment of the same model. The rest is sent for melting of steel to the nearby plants.

This equipment's performance is dependent on the following:

How close to perfection this equipment was reproduced.

Inherent defects are shared with new buyer/user so that they are able to resolve reoccurring problems.

Efficiency of this equipment is generally not more than 40 to 60% unless very carefully assembled.

Lebanon is a big market of old Mercedes cars and the country as a whole is well equipped to repair old Mercedes cars. One can see all over the place old cars working very efficiently. Even drivers are knowledgeable enough to carry out emergency repairs on the roadside, diagnose defects fast and swiftly move to nearby repair workshops before the car stops.

Dubai, for long, has been the biggest market for reconditioned Caterpillar earthmoving equipment.

Similarly, many major equipment producers have their designated dumping locations of old equipment and create adequate repair and maintenance facilities including spares for efficient operations before the equipment becomes redundant and goes for melting.

Ships and barges

Bhavnagar in Gujarat is one of the biggest ships-breaking markets in India. There are also many small sites including Mazagaon in Mumbai where ship-breaking activities are executed.

These are sea beach locations where ships are brought and grounded. These places have well-to-do and very efficient facilities to break ships in small components with proper diagnosis and repair facilities for all its equipment.

Their steel body is cut properly in standard sizes and sold for fabrication of structures.

Cut pieces of steel are sent to nearby steel re-rolling mills for melting and making steel bars for construction.

Ship engines, boilers, air-conditioning equipment, navigation equipment, etc. are carefully removed, serviced and repaired if possible and sold in the secondary market of spare parts either as equipment as a whole or parts like gearbox, piston sets, etc., for repairs of running ships.

Furniture, sometimes, fetches a very good price from people interested in antique furniture.

03 ⣿

Civil Engineering

Now, let us deliberate contracting as a civil engineering contractor and understand first the technical side and then the commercial side of it—it is very simple.

The following chapters demonstrate how humans, right from the pre-stone age, just by having a sense of needing improvement in living conditions by their innovative skills, have brought the world to this stage of living.

Let us understand and appreciate that none other than humans are provided with the abilities and qualities of intuition, innovation and implementation by the almighty; the supreme power. All other creatures are prospering on human's support. **Let's not let our life go to waste and do something good for the future of all.**

Even if your children are more intelligent than you, you have paved the way for future success/developments in many fields of life for your children.

Intuition is the ability to understand or know/think something new with/without conscious reasoning.

Innovation is the action/process of introducing a new idea or method for doing a job. The process for creating a new product is also called innovation.

Invention is a newly-created device or process.

The Chinese had a big number of labour forces working in a South Pacific country. Rice being their daily meal was imported at high costs. They had an **intuition** to grow rice locally and with their **innovative** methods, they found the variety of rice that could be grown locally. They developed methods of cultivation. Soon, the country became self-sufficient for rice production and locals also started eating rice; they never had even seen rice earlier.

An Indian entrepreneur had the **intuition** that all the steel is produced in East India while major consumption is in North and West India. Hence, he decided to have a steel manufacturing plant on the west coast. With **innovative efforts** with his team, he did set up Asia's biggest sponge iron plant on Gujarat's coast, successfully. They shipped iron ore, the raw material, from the east through their own ships and availed gas for heating and processing to convert iron ore into iron from the next-door ONGC facility in Hazira, Gujarat. The government readily provided land at a suitable location.

Production of heat, electricity, the light bulb, steam engines, floatation, etc., are **inventions** by humans.

3.1 What is civil engineering?

Civil engineering is a profession that deals with design, construction, and maintenance of the civic and living comforts and has been in existence from prehistoric ages.

Civil engineering was developed concurrent to or second only to military engineering, the oldest science of hunting, and protection from wild creatures and war with rivals.

Civil engineering has been a skill and process to physically build shelters and develop civilization so as to bring more comfort to life and save humans and other creatures dear to them from natural calamities and destruction.

Whatever improvements humans could think of were executed by intuitions and innovative methods to build something new as desired and called an 'invention.'

Initially, there were caves and shelters under trees. Slowly, they developed into thrashed huts and later elevated platforms to protect from insects, wild animals, landslides, rains and floods.

By 7, 000 BC, people had learned to make houses with mud mortar. They used thick mud paste to plaster walls made with tree branches and leaves. Sand paste was used to make the floors smooth. The rise of agriculture made permanent houses possible. Doorways were made on the roof, with ladders positioned both on the inside and outside of the houses. This protected them from rainwater, reptiles and other insects entering the houses at ground level. The roof was supported by beams of wood logs from the inside. Rough ground was covered by platforms, mats and skins on which residents slept.

The Great Wall of China was initially built in the same period, by putting mud plaster on a combination of tree branches and leaves.

With the passage of time, humans learnt to build houses with burnt bricks with windows for ventilation and illumination with sunlight, roads and drainage.

Water reservoirs, community centres, market places, grain-storage silos, etc. came into existence slowly.

The world's first sanitation system was found in India 3000 BC.

The world's first dockyard for building large boats and ships was built in India around 3000 BC. There used to be timber ships with several sails that were used to travel across continents with the support of wind energy.

The Indus Valley civilization was a major milestone of remarkable development in civil engineering of its time, in 2600–1900 BC.

The Indus Valley civilization was a major and important milestone in the development of civil engineering as per available information. Its centre was the city of Mohenjo-Daro. The city consisted of two parts. In the middle part was a citadel. It contained a public bath and assembly halls. It also held a granary where grain was stored. Streets on the outer parts of the town were laid in a grid pattern. The houses had 2 or even 3 stories and were made of brick as stone was uncommon in the area. Bricks were of a standard size and the Indus Valley civilization had standard weights and measures. Streets had networks of drainage.

Grain silos, the circular structure

The world's oldest university, Takshashila, was built in 700 BC in central India.

Till then and even thereafter, knowledge was transferred to young students by teaching on a one-to-one basis or in small groups in classrooms and while working.

From the above illustrations, it is obvious that one had addressed the task, thought properly, and planned with innovative ideas supported by previous experiences and then executed. This has always been a system, ever since the Stone Age and even now, this is the way many expert engineers/professionals address a difficult task.

With the advancement of knowledge, its compilation in books and computer-supported programs, we are now able to store our knowledge in a systematic manner and this knowledge could be used by future generations for their own applications and further developments/improvements.

Now, an engineer analyses the behaviour of any structure when subjected to its own weight and external forces including loads subjected by men and nature like winds and earthquakes, etc. to understand it. He now creates economical designs by providing adequate strengths in areas needing reinforcements and support.

Old structures were built with thick walls, big arches for roofs of buildings and doorway openings. Heavy timber logs were used for supporting big, flat building slabs and roofs. On top of these logs, thick stone slabs were laid, which were then topped up with a thin layer of plaster.

With proper placements of rock pieces in the form of bricks and slabs, big arches and domes could be built without any steel bars as it is even now seen in modern places of worship and other buildings.

Take a thin stick or branch of a plant. Hold the ends firmly and put some load on the stick. It will bend or break soon. Now, take a similar stick, bend it in the form of an arch and load on top of arch. Now, the same stick will take much higher loads and stand on its own. Such innovative logic is used in this profession.

Profiles of arches are developed with similar concepts, with the crown mostly being a wedge-shaped stone/brick to distribute loads on both sides along the profile of the arch.

Now, with the advancement of engineering knowledge and the availability of computer-aided design tools, we are able to design very light and smart-looking structures as per our requirements and intuitions.

Still, there is a gap. We are not able to easily reproduce some of the wonders built by our ancestors as the knowledge could not be preserved and died with them; it's difficult to recover. Some of our old monuments are standing for centuries with mysteries surrounding how they designed light and acoustics effects, erected delicate carvings at big heights and many other stunning features. All of them have been standing for centuries, having beaten nature.

3.2 NOW

Civil engineering is traditionally broken into many sub-disciplines of engineering works like roads, bridges, canals, dams, ports, buildings, industries, public health engineering, etc. Basic knowledge in these disciplines is taught in engineering institutions.

Civil engineering takes place in the public sector from municipal through to national governments, and in the private sector, from individual homeowners through to international design and construction companies to build mega-projects across the world.

04

Execution of Initial Construction Contracts

In the earlier chapters, we have deliberated small subcontracts executed as per directions/requirements of the project engineers.

Now, we deliberate how a contractor starts a new engineering contract and does his business.

Until around 1960, experienced contractors were given government contracts in India on the basis of their past experience and resources but there were a few major accidents.

There was a river bridge under construction in eastern Uttar Pradesh around 1960. Soon after removing supports, the bridge collapsed. The contractor swiftly removed all of his equipment, materials and workers from site before the government engineer could report it to the police.

When questioned in court, the contractor expressed his total ignorance in technical matters and stated that he was working as per the directions of the government engineers, thus making them totally responsible for the accident. After a few such incidences, it became mandatory in India for contractors to post a well-qualified and experienced engineer at site, responsible for the project's execution.

Now, it is mandatory that not only the contractor must appoint a qualified engineer, his resume should be to the satisfaction of the client and approved by them before the beginning of the contract, depending upon complexity and size of the job.

While tendering for a project, the contractor needs to demonstrate some experience in the execution of similar projects and his resources intending to deploy on project, including men, equipment, money and experience on similar jobs. For experience, he may take another company as partner for the particular project.

He could also take a major subcontract from a big contractor for the first job to save himself from meeting the elaborate qualification criteria.

Alternatively, start small.

A person looks for a medium to large-size project in his vicinity. He visits nearby construction projects a few times and tries to understand what is happening and develops an interest to do something on the project. In the process, he develops a few acquaintances.

Most of the projects have some easy areas which the main contractor will be willing to give away to small vendors, allowing him to concentrate on more vital issues. They are even willing to support technically and provide skeleton superintendence and equipment. **This fills in the gap in place of previous experience.**

With his intelligence, he approaches key persons intending to sublet works in a few specific areas. After some introductory discussions, a small test order is placed. On successful completion of this small job, he is paid. He makes some money and gets a bigger job. **This is the start of a contractor's business. Depending on his capabilities, interest and quality output, he grows fast and become a successful contractor.**

05

Factors to Be Foreseen/ Considered While Taking the Decision of Whether or Not to Accept a Construction Contract

1. Does the client have the capacity and the willingness to pay after the job is done?

2. Is the job politically motivated?

3. Local conditions and hostilities?

4. Weather conditions?

5. Logistic conditions?

6. Construction time schedule?

7. Technical capability of the contractor?

8. Is the job doable under the given circumstances?

9. Availability of resources.

10. Does it require capital investment?

11. **What is the return on capital on this job?**

12. **Any guarantees required by the owner before award of the contract?**

13. **Financial capabilities and supports?**

14. **Contingencies?**

15. **Net earnings after taxes**

16. **Possibility of getting further jobs concurrent to finishing this job?**

5.1 Does the client have the capacity and willingness to pay after the job is done?

Almost all clients have cash flow problems on a construction project due to some reason or the other. But still, if he has honest intentions and the capacity to pay bills on or around due dates, he is considered a good client. There could be problems such as:

Delay in clearance of financial support from investors/banks and their disbursement.

Most of the new projects are funded by a financial institution/bank. These banks invest about 60% to 80% of the cost of the project and the balance is to be funded by the developer/entrepreneur.

Generally, while the application for bank funding is in process, the developer starts the project with his share of the money. This also provides more confidence to the investor and the loan process becomes easier.

In cases of delays by banks, the clients will not be able to pay off their dues to the contractor. With this delay/stoppage, the contractor's cash flow also gets strained and he faces a dilemma as to how long he should continue with the project using his own money. The contractor should not feel shy; he is not there to fund the client's business. He could help the client out by continuing the work while straining his cash flow to a comfortable extent suitable to him upon production of **cashable guarantees** and interest payments by the client.

In many such situations, the client enjoys at the cost of the contractor and many contractors go bankrupt. Such situations must be avoided. With his own resources, the contractor should always have knowledge of the status on funding of the project.

Expenses on the project are more than estimated

This happens when the client becomes over-ambitious and starts new additions of facilities without any provisions in the budget or when the original budget is wrong. This is very dangerous if the client knows about the good financial capabilities of the contractor. The contractor must take remedial measures before getting into this trap. The following measures could be explored.

If the client is a private firm, an irrevocable bank guarantee for an amount equal to a few months' billing could be taken from them. If the client does not pay within a reasonable period of time, money could be taken from the bank on presentation of the guarantee.

In high-rise commercial and residential buildings, generally, a joint account between the owner and contractor is opened in the bank. All receipts are received in this account and the developer gets the remaining amount after adjustment of the contractor's bills.

If work gets stuck halfway and contractor is interested to help, he purchases a few flats at negotiated cheaper rates and completes the building instead of paying for these flats. He recovers his money by selling these flats.

For government projects, some solution is found depending on situation by discussions but contractor should not feel shy in talking. Nobody would help if damage is done.

Bill payments are delayed towards end of the project and special conditions

Initially, the client makes quick payments to get the work to progress fast but towards the end, due to various reasons, he usually starts delaying and the contractor, being stuck on the project, must somehow finish the job.

The last bill is generally delayed since all the accounts and free supplies by the client in the contract are once again checked for any mistakes or omissions—a time-taking exercise. Hence, it is up to the contractor's skills that the last bill is made as small as possible, and all the payments are released in normal course before completing the job.

A big contractor was doing a submarine pipeline job, about a kilometre along the sea bed for a known industrialist. By mistake, his engineer scheduled a big sum in the payment schedule that was to be paid after the job was completed. The industrialist first delayed the payment of the last bill for about a year and then, on the intervention of common friends, the contractor could ultimately recover only a part of the payment—that too in a few instalments that extended to almost two more years.

On another government contract for the construction of a big river bridge, just before completion of the bridge, government funds were diverted to some important defence projects. Government officials called for a meeting with the contractor. The contractor politely explained that he has already recovered his profits on the job and is doing the rest of the job on a cash loss. Hence, cancelling the contract would not be of any benefit to the government. They agreed to continue the work and finish the bridge with extended payment terms agreed upon in the meeting with the contractor.

On a prestigious large-construction contract in difficult logistics and political atmosphere for a big, multinational company, there was a condition in the contract that in case the owner was not able to pay in time, the contractor would still complete the job on time, without any delay, with his own financial resources.

The contractor had put 40% of the contract amount as contingency fund available to the project manager and completed the job without any difficulty. Further, there was an extra price built in the contract for the purpose.

In another government contract, 15% mobilization advance was payable at the start of the project on providing a bank guarantee of the like amount and further, a 12% advance was payable on hypothecation of construction equipment after their arrival at site. All these advances were recoverable in instalments starting after 25% work was completed. A contractor was happy and quoted aggressively for the project but did not read the complete tender document and missed that all these advances were 18% interest-bearing, and the interest was compounded on a monthly basis. The contractor purchased a lot of new equipment and happily spent the entire advance, resulting in serious cash flow problems, delays and losses due to heavy recovery of advances and interest thereon towards the end of the project.

The same contractor finished many jobs for the same client with good profits by restricting advances and disciplined cash flows.

The contractor must read all the conditions very carefully and price the contract accordingly. In any case, if the contract conditions or reputation of the client are not favourable, it would be advised to avoid pursuing such a contract at competitive prices.

5.2 Is the job politically motivated?

Political motivation is of two types.

- Too many politicians show interest of support

- Government decides to execute some contracts for their political gains.

5.2.1 Too many politicians show interest of support

Construction contracts have extensive public dealings. Hence, the contractor must understand sentiments and expectations of the public, the local administration and politicians. They all could be a big support at a price.

An engineer went for a pre-tender survey for a big road contract in a disturbed area.

News of his being in town spread like wildfire. Many local politicians and others who may matter in dealing with the public for the execution of this contract sought appointments with this engineer to commit their solidarity and support in case of the award of contract to his company. He quoted three times the normal price but still, he was not the highest price bidder.

5.2.2 Government decides to execute some contracts for their political gains.

In a democratic country, the governments keep on changing and different political parties come to power.

New governments, with their own agenda of governance, start infrastructure and other projects in specific fields and areas.

Once a new government is formed, many new projects are announced and executed. It is always preferred to get involved in the contracts which will be completed within the tenure of that government. The next government may or may not support such projects, adversely affecting all the contractors engaged in such projects.

One government announced many road projects throughout the country soon after its formation. It was a big boom and, in addition to good capacities of local contractors, a big fleet of contractors from overseas came to participate in this massive nation-building exercise. Soon, upon a change of government, policy changed and all the contracts that were half-finished lost their momentum.

5.3 Local conditions and hostilities?

The public around the project area could be hostile due to many reasons and, in all fairness, the client should share the potential problems with the contractors before deciding the price of the contract. Enough provision should be made in price to take care of these problems.

A project was to be executed in a deep forest with cannibal habitants. But however, no report of cannibalism was received for the past few years. The contractor was adequately briefed even before site visit and adequate safety measures were jointly taken for successful and timely completion of the project.

These habitats were treated respectfully and habitation centres were opened with good food and teachings. Teachers were also from the same community, who were sensible and willing to cooperate.

Movement out of the project security zone was fully restricted and possible under heavy police cover only. Otherwise, all movements were carried out by helicopters as far as possible.

Goods moved in convoys under security cover.

At the end of the project, everybody left with their good friends with them, safely. However, enough provisions of money were kept in the contract and the contractor spent all the necessary money with the administrative support of the client.

Confrontation is never the right solution in such cases where local habitats are trained to run the plant with skeleton supervision of experts.

Generally, in remote areas, people are poor and uneducated. A good lessoning while providing some comforts as per their requirement always gives good dividends.

In another case, the site was heavily prone to malaria. The contractor sprayed mosquito repellent chemicals regularly at site. Everybody took anti-malaria pills and wore mosquito repellent clothing. During the three-year contract period, there was no incidence of a worker falling sick due to malaria.

5.4 Weather conditions

For the execution of a construction contract, construction equipment and construction methods are to be carefully selected conducive to local weather conditions. Even more time, efforts and money would be required to execute a project in case of extreme weather conditions, especially rains and hot climate.

If daytime temperature reaches around or higher than 42-degree centigrade, long lunch breaks and night working is preferred to avoid physical work in the open sun while the temperature is highest to avoid dehydration and low productivity of workers. Water is sprinkled on concreting aggregates to make them cooler and ice is added to concrete while mixing in the batching plant. Alternatively, a water-chilling plant is supplemented to the concrete-batching plant to lower down the temperature of wet concrete during mixing and placements. Handling of steel bars and structural steel need more care and hand gloves, to avoid blisters in hands of workers, are provided. Wear and tear of tires of heavy vehicles is higher on hot roads.

Water content in wet concrete and loose earth used to making earthen bunds and embankments is important and has to be controlled. Hence, enough care has to be taken to control water content while it is raining—especially in frequent and heavily rainy-weather conditions. During seasonal rains, work is suspended. But in tropical countries, where it rains throughout the year, special methods of earthwork, concreting and asphalt work are carried out in protected environments. Tarpaulins are spread and makeshift sheds are erected to avoid mixing of rainwater.

In extreme cold, working is comparatively better and some chemicals are added for early setting of concrete, asphalt etc.

5.5 Logistic conditions

Sometimes, procurement and movement of men and material for a construction project is a challenge due to the location and surroundings of the project.

Often contractors, without proper visit of site and study, land up in very difficult situations and lose a lot of money and time to overcome difficulties.

One such fairly difficult site was as under:

There was a natural gas exploration and production site more than 1000 Km from the nearest seaport, amidst the dense rainforest and only a single-road track was available with hostile tribes living along the road.

Contract provisions indicated the construction of a proper road in the entire length of the approach, with proper gradients for transport of heavy and bulky equipment included in the scope of work of the developer of an oil field.

This job changed a few hands due to poor logistic conditions. Ultimately, the entrepreneur, who completed the project suggested building an airport at his cost and giving the airport to government after completing his mobilization instead of making the road.

The government was cooperative and an airport to handle even the biggest cargo aircrafts in the world was built at the site in three years, to bring equipment by air to the site. In addition, some roads were upgraded for ease movement of construction material from nearest smaller airport for construction of this airport.

Author has done the mistake for taking construction contract for part of this airport without proper study of logistics. It was a surprise when he made his first aerial visit by a helicopter and landed at site before mobilization for the job. It was nothing but dense forest with practically no habitation. Even things like material for cooking food were to be imported.

Roads were graded with many potholes and very steep gradients needing high power trucks and trailers. Tires could not last more than 5000 kilometres.

For safety, all trucks and employees used to travel in convoys with armed security escorts.

Being a resourceful contractor, the project was completed on time and the client also reasonably compensated for the extra expenses on the project due to unforeseen, difficult logistics.

5.6 Time to complete the project.

All projects have different utilities after completion and they can be classified into two broad classifications.

- There are certain projects that should be completed on time but extra resources should not be deployed to finish the project early, i.e., the client is not willing to compensate for the early finishing of the project—rather, he does not mind if reasonably-extra time is spent to save some costs to the project.

- Time-bound projects' completion is important to the client since his further activities have to start soon after this part of the project is completed. He does not mind if some extra money is spent for the early finishing of the project or very heavy penalty is charged for delays.

Generally, infrastructure projects provide comfortable time for completion. As a standard practice, they charge 10% of the price of the balance work remaining unfinished by the agreed date of completion subject to a maximum limit of 5% of the contract value. Further, they also give extensions of time for completion of the project due to certain unavoidable circumstances.

In time-bound projects, time is an important factor—rather, the substance of many contracts—for completing the project by a specified date. The client may have planned to start his next activity or to start production in his facility after project completion. He does all the investment at high-interest costs and rigs up a big establishment. Even in some cases, he makes forward commitments of delivery of his products, produced by the project after its completion.

The client, in such cases, is willing to pay a reasonably-high price for the job but would not accept any delays or compromise on the quality of the job. A contractor having a reputation of delivering jobs on time is even invited and the job is awarded on mutual discussions at a comfortably-high price with firm commitments.

On one such high-priority job, in very difficult logistic and physical conditions and heavy rains on a regular basis:

- The client asked contractors to mobilize resources to complete the project in eighteen months while he had an internal schedule to be completed in three years. There were unavoidable delays in the start of the project for more than six months due to some technical problems related to daily rain around the year and approval of suitable construction methods in such adverse conditions. The client agreed to pay for all the idling and cost of additional resources provided the job was completed as per his schedule.

- They engaged a group of three contractors from different countries—each one of the best in their respective country, with well-defined scope of works for each contractor and a condition that if anyone is lagging in his progress, the others would step up and complete his job without any extra cost to the client.

- They provided very good logistic support at the disposal of the contractors on a need basis.

- They completed the contract and commissioned the facility just before time and saved high idling costs of production facilities and honoured commitments of supplies to his customers which are much more important than other parameters for timely finishing of the project.

Beginners must be very careful and should not land in time-bound work assignments. After doing a few jobs and getting confidence, if the job is within reach and at a comfortable price, time-bound jobs can be taken with proper planning and understanding.

Sensible clients also do not engage unreliable contractors for such jobs under any circumstances.

5.7 Technical capability of the contractor

In the interest of the project, it is very important that the contractor has the capabilities and resources to execute the project.

Consultant to the project, working with client/owner, designs the engineering process to be used for the project, its sourcing, specifications, quality parameters, etc., and prepares a list of difficult areas to be addressed with time and cost estimates. The consultant does preliminary investigations at the site of work, basic engineering, procurement, construction specifications and conditions of the contract. This includes safety and logistic challenges, project-time schedule, quantities of work to be executed and payment terms.

These proposals and documents are discussed with the client and necessary changes are made as per the advice and agreements of the consultant.

Often, clients get these proposals from a few consultants and select one considered to be the best.

Now, the consultant prepares an enquiry document for bidding by contractors and circulated either by public bidding or on invitation to a few contractors.

Contractors submit their bids in two sealed packets—one called technical bid and the other called the price bid.

First, technical bids are opened and a few contractors are selected, who have requisite capabilities. Some of them even provide alternatives to consultant's proposals for the choice of client/consultants.

Detailed discussions are held by the client and the consultants with all the selected contractors, on the following issues.

- Past experience on doing similar jobs

- Method statement—how will he execute the job

- Explain to client's satisfaction that he understands the job and does have the capability to execute it without any problem

- List of resources including experts and equipment to be mobilized

- Manpower deployment schedule

- Time schedule for execution

- Selection of project manager—his personal interview by consultants and approvals

- Financial capabilities and banking support for cash flow

- Special conditions of contract, asked by contractor

- Special conditions anticipated by the consultant/client.

- Etc.

A few contractors are finally selected and financial preferences are decided by the client even before opening the price bids.

The contract is awarded to the techno-commercially lowest bidder after opening the prices of **approved contractors only.** In such cases, the selected contractor may not be the lowest-price bidder. Even the prices for non-technically qualified contractors are not opened and the sealed price cover is returned to the contractor.

For a tender of construction of some specialized industrial plant, the lowest bidder was technically rejected and the second-lowest contractor was recommended for award by the engineering team of the owner. The lowest price bidder proposed a single payment only on successful completion of the contract, i.e., **no satisfaction, no pay.** He was awarded the job. Such gimmicks do work very well if used at the right opportunities.

5.8 Is the job doable under the given circumstances?

Often, the contractor plunges into a difficult job out of overconfidence or sheer frustration. This is very dangerous, especially for beginners and many well-experienced contractors lose heavily; it could even become threat to the very existence of the business.

We have sighted this true example of a project in Oman in the year 1979 in Para 1.03, where the management was able to save the company through a change in management.

Neither did the company have the necessary work experience nor the proper management staff. They did not have any job and in desperation, they picked up two jobs—one about 600 km at Hima and another at Fahud oil fields of Petroleum Development of Oman. Difficult logistics added to their problems and they could not do well on both the jobs. Hence, it forced the promoters to change the management.

Fahud oil field project was one-year project with unlimited liquidated damages levied at certain percentage of the value of the unfinished job after expiry of contract period, on monthly basis, and the contractor has just finished 30% of job after expiry of two years.

Instead of closing down the business, the promoters decided to try changing the management.

The new management showed good progress within one month of their physical involvement and offered to complete the job within five months if all the liquidated damages were waived. Petroleum Development of Oman agreed instantly to waive off all the liquidated damages with a condition that the same would be levied as per contract if there was a delay of even one day after the agreed-upon completion date of the project.

It was a good option for the client since it would have taken much more time to complete the contract if they'd changed the contractor.

The contractor deployed three times the number of resources needed in his opinion and saved the company by finishing the job four days before the agreed-upon completion date in spite of fifteen days' delay in some imports. This time period included motivation and training of the existing workforce of mixed nationalities. Alternative of mobilization of a new skilled workforce was not possible in such a short time.

A contractor with a confident and dedicated team is always chosen to do only difficult jobs at his price and get very good reputation and profits.

It is not only confidence that is important to execute difficult jobs but also the knowledge and capacity to mobilize additional resources if required. One learns while working and often has to change their method of execution which may require additional resources and increase costs with no loss of time.

5.9 Availability of resources

Availability of resources is a big consideration for selection of a contract by any contractor.

If resources are not readily available with the contractor, they would be either hired or procured new/second-hand and enough provisions are to be kept in pricing of the contract. A comfortable price is quoted provided the contractor is still willing to make investments in new purchases and increase inventory in his resource lists.

If all the resources like construction equipment, skilled manpower, engineers and knowhow for the particular project are readily available or would be available soon, the contractor quotes a very keen price, making compromises on equipment rentals, etc., on the project costing. Quoting low is a serious issue and should be avoided.

He should not quote very low prices so as to avoid regrets after taking up the project. Often, he gets another project of similar nature at a good price soon after getting the project and naturally, he diverts his attention and resources to the new project and this project suffers losses and delays.

Many times, the management does not even quote for the tender due to paucity of resources and other constraints/commitments.

5.10 Does it require capital investment?

Capital investment, if required for a new job, should be checked from all the angles, including bare necessities, returns of investment from the job and future utility of the investment. An efficient engineer/contractor finds workable solutions and tries to execute the job with the available resources with least capital investment. He could hire some equipment for short periods. Investments not giving desired returns or becoming liabilities after the end of job should be avoided even at the cost of not taking the contract.

5.11 Return on capital on this job?

Even if investment is made on a new job one must ensure reasonably good return of investment on this job itself. If investment is fully charged on the project without compromising with cash profits, it is better to invest instead of hiring of equipment on the project.

All equipment hirers provide vehicles on basis of recovery of investment in three years and heavy equipment with less wear and tear on the basis of returns in ten years. Hence if contractor has confirmed usage for longer periods, he should invest instead of hiring equipment.

5.12 Any guarantees required by the owner before award of contract?

Ina large contract, generally following bank guaranties/insurances from reputed insurance companies are required by the client/owner from the contractor. However, a few of these guarantees are not required by the owner for smaller and simpler contracts.

- Bank guarantee from an approved bank for 10% of contract value for the duration of the contract, including maintenance period for **performance** by the contractor according to the contract, **called a performance bank guarantee must be obtained.**

- **Working capital** required for running the project.

- Bank guarantee for the amount in case of any **advance payments** given by the owner for starting the job

- Bank guarantee for any advances taken by the contractor against the **material in stock** at the project site. This guarantee may be needed if the material at site is not secured—like road projects.

- **Hypothecation** of equipment in favour of the client if any advances are taken for the mobilization of construction equipment. Equipment cannot move out till the job is finished and all advances are cleared.

- **Contractor's all-risk insurance** for any damages to work, floods washouts and accidents during construction of the project to the value of a minimum of 10% of the contract value to be mandatorily taken before the start of the job. This will also cover losses to client's personnel working on project to be insured for values specified by the client.

- In hostile areas with possibilities of war damages, specific inclusion for cover for hostilities and war damages are to be made in the contractor's all-risk policy with enhanced insurance premium.

- **Insurance** against accidents to be taken for the duration of the contract for all the workers.

- **Insurance** for all the equipment deployed on job against accidents is mandatory if equipment is hypothecated with the owner.

- Accident and medical insurance for **senior executives** as per terms of their employment. Some senior executives, like project directors and specialist consultants, ask for adequate insurance cover for themselves in their employment contracts.

- Equipment-in-transit insurance.

- Materials in transit insurance.

- Etc.

For EPC (Engineering, procurement and construction) contracts, the contractor's engineering department/consultant for the project should take insurance for value of the project valid from the start of the project to the end of the defect liability period of the project as per contract, indemnifying the client against any defects in engineering and design of the project. This insurance is called **professional indemnity** to be provided by the design engineer. This indemnity is required from the contractor only if the project design is in his scope. Otherwise, if the client has appointed some engineering consultant, this indemnity insurance will be arranged for by the consultant. In India, such insurance is provided by New India Insurance Company after a thorough check on resources including experienced engineers, design tools and past experience.

With all these bank guarantees and insurances, the **client is fully secured** against any adverse eventuality.

Banks and insurance companies ask for adequate security from the company before issuing guarantees. They have to pay on first demand irrespective of if there are funds available in the contractor's bank accounts or not.

For their reputation and continuation of business, owners make sure their bank guarantees are never cashed.

The contractor must assure himself that he has adequate resources including knowhow, past experience, expert manpower including engineers with relevant experience, immovable assets which could be pledged to banks and, above all, self-confidence before taking up a mega-challenging project.

It is not that simple to take a contract including engineering of a project, without a proper engineering set up that is up to the satisfaction of the client.

On one such project being executed by the owner by directly employing a construction team, one young engineer opted to design a building. He was permitted to design but the design was vetted by an engineering consultant of the owner's choice for a fee, before the start of construction. The consultant took the responsibility of stability of the structure.

As per international practice, all engineering consultants, for their own safety and the comfort of their clients, take sufficient insurance cover against their professional indemnity and keep on adding new projects to this policy on awards and deleting after they are complied.

5.13 Financial capabilities and supports.

We have just deliberated different types of bank guarantees, capital investments, working capital and insurance covers are required for undertaking major construction projects on contracts. All these require good and reliable financial support in terms of investments in movable and immovable property.

Insurance companies, banks and other financial institutions look for something cashable in their control, in cases of difficulties and these institutions have to bailout money on demand by the client and other agencies against guarantees they have provided to them on behalf of the contractor.

As the contractor's business grows and he moves forward to take bigger and bigger challenges, he has to create assets by investments in office, heavy equipment and fixed deposits with banks. Investment in one's own house is generally the first thing to pledge but it should be the last item to be pledged to any financial institution. The bank taking over someone's house is itself very depressing.

If contractor has a good track record of paying back loans and advances on time, he gets many relaxations in providing securities.

For a good contractor and for reputed client, loans are even given for working capital against contractors' bills. The client pays to designated accounts of the contractor and the bank releases money after recovering his agreed percentage of bill payment or fixed instalments.

5.14 Contingencies

Adequate provisions are to be made in the contract for unforeseen events/happenings/expenses on the project, called contingencies.

Client's contingencies

Clients generally keep provisions for contingencies in payment schedules as an item generally called *provisional sums*. In provisional sums, a certain amount of money is provided to be spent on instructions of clients for additional works not included in the contract. In some contracts, provisional sums are also termed as client's contingencies.

Contractor's contingencies,

The contractor, while submitting his bid to the client, prices the project work for the scope of the work described in the contract and general conditions of the contract given in the tender document. Before closing the price bid, he has to think of the possibilities of hidden or unaccounted expenses he may have to incur during the contract period and adds them together to put in as contingencies in his pricing schedule. These contingencies are added to the price by distributing them on certain items of works of his choice.

These extra costs could be due to the following reasons:

Time overruns

If contractor feels that the time for execution of contract is insufficient and he may not finish the job within the time allotted in the tender, he submits the tender to complete the job in the time allotted but adds for the following costs in his bid:

- Liquidated damages he may have to pay for time overruns.

- Extra expenses on overheads, wages and equipment hire and other costs during the extended period of stay on the project.

Social welfare expenses

Such expenses are common in projects in remote areas. However, their extent differs from project to project. Such costs should be carefully estimated and added to the project price.

Security

Pre-tender investigation team should correctly assess local attitudes and behaviour towards outsiders and requirement of security for safe movement of the contractor's men and material. This is in addition to safety and security measures normally taken on a project site.

On one of the projects, after getting the contract and mobilization to the site, it was realized that all the material and workforce had to necessarily move under heavy security escorts. This not only increased the costs but also caused delays, fear and the absence of a carefree work environment adversely affected work efficiency. There was always a threat of looting and harassments in cases of stoppage of vehicles due to any reasons. Adequate cover has to be made in pricing for such eventualities, if suspected. However, this happens in very rare cases.

Corruption and bribery

It is difficult to find any place where a fully honest work environment is in existence. All places have it, the only difference being that ways of taking and giving favours and their costs are different. Now, for on cost estimates, there is a separate column termed as *business expenses* where these costs, with adequate provisions, are provided for.

On one of the territories, such costs used to be 40% of the contract price, i.e., if the cost is 40, 40 would be expenses and 20 would be the profit before tax. Hence, the price would be 2.5 times the actual cost.

In one of the tenders in a different territory, a contractor requested the client to disqualify him since he was unable to satisfy their expectations unless he was allowed to increase the price. They wanted firm commitments and in return, were only willing to provide assistance if circumstances were favouring them, with no risks. One should never accept such a gamble unless they are very confident.

A contractor, hand-in-gloves with the client, quoting low prices just to get the contract is a different case. They put some conditions in the tender, who will escalate the price during execution and the client, willingly or unaware, ignores these conditions.

On a major seaport project, a contractor put a condition in his tender that the rates were based on the condition that suitable rock will be available within 40 km from project site. And any haulage from a longer distance will be paid extra at certain rates specified in his document. Rock in the near vicinity was rejected and everybody made good money on extra payments on long haulages for the rocks—the biggest items in the contract.

For marine construction, rock is used in various sizes including big boulders of specified minimum weights for foundations and counter effect of water waves and currents. Hence, quality of rock is important and its specifications should not be compromised on.

- Rock should be heavy with greater specific gravity for better stability in water with heavy currents.

- It should not have weak joints—joints will open with passage of time and rock will break into pieces.

- It should not be abrasive. Else, with the beating of water, waves will wear it out soon.

An honest client would at least expect good behaviour, superior quality of work with expensive fittings and acceptance of his so-called small requests of additional works and modifications, etc. without any extra costs to him. All this cost is charged to the contractor's pocket.

Fixed time contracts with heavy liquidated damages in case of delays

Such contracts should have adequate provisions in contingencies for the following;

- Extra resources may be required to complete the job in time.

- Some provision for payment of liquidated damages

- If liquidated, damages are liable without limits. Enough precaution should be taken before deciding in favour of taking such contracts.

Variations in lump sum contracts

An international Engineering, Procurement and Construction contractor in Oman gave a civil works sub-contract to a local construction company with measured bill of quantities provided by him with a condition that this contract will be treated as a lump sum contract if the total variation in quantities is within certain +/- limits. The sub-contractor increased his price to an extent within these limits and in the end of the contract, everybody was happy with a fair deal. In the end, quantities were more than the prescribed limits and the contractor was paid extra as per the contract conditions.

In cases of lump-sum contracts, there should always be some contingency provision for increase in quantities due to whatever are the reasons.

There could be many more unforeseen circumstances and all these should be properly priced in the bid.

5.15 Net earnings after taxes

After all the conditions are considered, the contractor first takes a decision to bid for the job or not.

If he is still interested to bid, how serious he is in taking the job depends upon:

His total cost

His profit expectations

Price the job as per his parameters

The price at which the job should be available

He should never quote for any job for less profit or no profit. It is always better, in the long run, to lose the job instead of taking a job knowing that it may not make any profit.

There are fair ways to put some conditions in the tender document to cover your apprehensions due to which your price has been increased.

Figure out such apprehensions; put them nicely in your bid with a condition that in case this happens, the price would increase to this extent. For example:

- We have considered stone chips would be available at a distance of 15 kilometres from the site. In case the source of supply is more than 15 kilometres, the extra spent on stone chips will be paid at six rupees per tonne.

- We have not considered any import duty payable by us on import of construction material. In case of any duty levied, we would be reimbursed at actual plus 25% to cover our overheads and profit.

After these conditions, the price may be suitably adjusted without sacrificing your profits/earnings.

We will deliberate these issues in a later part of this book in detail, once the other parameters are explained for major contracts.

5.16 Possibility of getting further jobs concurrent to finishing this job?

While entering a new territory or new types of jobs, it should always be considered whether the job is doable with a risk of entering some unknown parameters and then why should we take the risk.

Executives interested in taking the job try to sell the idea that many jobs would be available after completing the contract. This should be examined thoroughly without any bias and instead of depending only on one executive; more investigation should be carried out to the satisfaction of the management.

Even if the job is taken, a low price should not be quoted. If a low price is quoted, firstly it becomes difficult to complete the job and further, once the job is completed at low profits, the management usually conveniently forgets the earlier considerations for quoting low and even decides not to venture in that territory further.

One chief executive changed his job from Singapore (name changed) to a different country. He walked in with a job in Singapore for this company with an assurance of getting many more jobs in Singapore with his influences and everybody in this new company was happy. In desperation of getting the contract, he quoted very low and thus, the company had to lose heavily. This chief executive lost his job and, moreover, the promoter's confidence was shaken and he refused similar jobs even at good prices in Singapore.

It is always good to venture into areas where further jobs are available but never at the cost of the first job. The first job should always have comfortable margins. Further, in the first job, there are usually many unforeseen problems which eat away some of the profits

06 ▪▪▪ ▪▪▪ ▪▪▪

Building Materials

6.1 Earthwork

Unlike soil for agriculture, soil for construction work should be free of organic materials, manure, vegetation and other impurities. Soils with organic impurities fail faster and are hence to be avoided in building foundations, high banks and road construction.

During construction work, the soil on top of the ground—which is generally organic in nature and good for agriculture—should be removed, stored in a separate place and spread in green belts after completing foundations and roads of the project. It should not be wasted.

Soil free of organic and other impurities, commonly known as earth, is extensively used in the construction of structural foundations, earthen dams, roads and high banks for different purposes.

It is important that earth should be strong and capable enough to take the loads of equipment, foundations and high bank; it should not settle/ shrink or distort while it's loaded according to its capacity. Else, it may damage the structure.

While walking, if one puts his feet in wet soil, due to high water content in the soil—and if the water content increases further—he may even sink in the earthen pond called 'marshy land.' Water content in soil plays an important role in the strength of earthen structures.

Depending on the quantity of water present in earthen mass, it behaves in four ways.

- Loose soil, when water content is less than OMC and it is not compacted properly with air pockets, shrinks on application of load.

- Compacted soil is good for structural load when the water content is as per OMC and is adequately compacted.

- As water content increases, its load-bearing capacity reduces and, eventually, it reaches the plastic stage of not being capable of taking any load; this is commonly called mud.

- On further increase in water content, soil starts flowing freely in a liquid state, as commonly seen in swamps.

Water content at a stage where the soil can be compacted to its maximum density/highest load-bearing capacity is called Optimum Moisture Content (OMC). Similarly, for the start of plastic state, water content is called plastic limit and it is called liquid limit for turning into liquid state. All these stages could be determined in field laboratory by simple tests.

Density is weight of any mass per unit of volume, i.e., 2.6 tonnes per cubic meter.

OMC is moisture content at which the soil can be compacted to highest density.

OMC for any soil is checked in field laboratory by a simple Modified Proctor Compaction Test.

6.1.1 Modified proctor compaction test

Modified Proctor Test is used to determine compaction of different types of soils by changing moisture content; a graph is plotted for density at different moisture contents. Moisture content for maximum density is considered as optimum moisture content.

To obtain relationship of the 'dry density' to 'moisture content' in the form of a compaction curve and for determining the values of Optimum Moisture Content (OMC) and Maximum Dry Density (MDD), modified proctor tests are carried out in field laboratories.

6.1.2 Apparatus required

1: Proctor Mould and Metal Rammer

Metal meld (volume = 1000 cm³ for 100 mm diameter meld and volume = 2250 cm³ for 150 mm diameter meld (as per IS: 10074-1982) and Metal rammer conforming to IS: 9189-1979. (Weight = 4.9 kg)

2: Balance

Balance: One of a capacity of 10 kg and least count 1 g and another of 200 g capacity and sensitivity of 0.01 g

3: Sieve

4.75 mm, 19 mm and 37.5 mm I.S. Sieves conforming to IS: 460 (Part 1) –1985

4: Oven

Thermostatically controlled to maintain temperature between 1050 to 1100°C

5: Steel Straight Edge

For trimming the protruded excessive soil of the mould

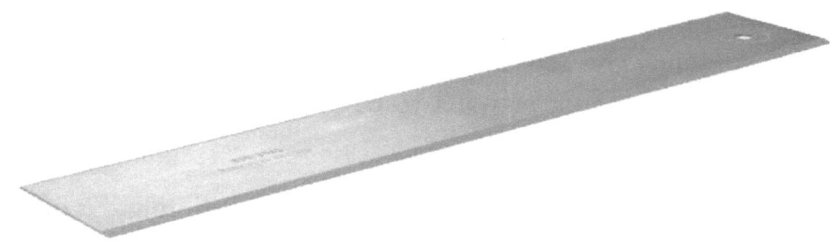

6: Airtight Container

For taking a sample for determination of Moisture Content

Reference

IS-2720 (Part-8):1983 (Reaffirmed – May 2015) "Methods of test for soils: Determination of water content – dry density relation using heavy compaction".

6.1.3 Procedure

1. Take a representative portion of air-dried soil large enough to provide about 5 kg of material passing 19 mm IS sieve (for soils not susceptible to crushing during compaction) or about 15 kg of material passing 19 mm IS sieve (for soils susceptible to crushing during compaction. Sieve them on a 19 mm sieve and then reject the coarse fraction of material.

2. Add a suitable amount of water to the soil and mix it thoroughly. For sandy and gravelly soil, add 3% to 5% of water. For cohesive soil, the amount of water to be added should be 12% to 16% below the plastic limit.

3. Weigh the mould with the base plate attached, round it off to the nearest 1 g and record the weight as W1. Attach the extension collar with the mould. Compact the moist soil into the mould in five layers of approximately equal mass, each layer being given

25 blows with the help of a 4.9 kg rammer, dropped from a height of 450 mm above the soil. The blows must be distributed uniformly over the surface of each layer.

The operator shall ensure that the tube of the rammer is kept clear of soil so that the rammer always falls freely.

4. After completion of the compaction operation, remove the extension collar and level carefully the top of the mould by means of a straightedge. Weigh the mould with the compacted soil to the nearest 1 gram and record this weight as W2.

5. Remove the compacted soil from the mould and place it on the mixing tray. Determine the water content of a representative sample of the specimen by heating. Record the moisture content as 'M'.

6. The remainder of the soil shall be broken up. Repeat steps (iii) to (v) above by adding suitable increment of water to the soil. For sandy and gravelly soils, the increment is generally 1% to 2% and for cohesive soils, the increment is generally 2% to 4%. The total number of determinations made shall be at least five and the moisture contents should be such that the optimum moisture content at which the maximum dry density occurs is within that range.

7. For compacting soil containing coarse material up to 37.5 mm size, the 2250 cm^3 mould should be used. A sample weighing about 30 kg and passing the 37.5 mm IS sieve is used for the test. Soil is compacted in five layers, with each layer being given 55 blows of the 4.9 kg rammer.

It is important that the water is mixed thoroughly and adequately with the soil since inadequate mixing gives rise to variable test results. This is particularly important with cohesive soils when adding a substantial quantity of water to the air-dried soil. With clays of high plasticity, or where hand mixing is employed, it may be difficult to distribute the water uniformly through the air-dried soil by mixing alone It may be required that the mixed sample is stored in a sealed container for a minimum period of about 16 hours before continuing with the test.

It is necessary to control the total volume of the soil compacted since it has been found that if the amount of soil struck off after removing the extension is too much, the test results will be inaccurate.

Water added for each stage of the test should be such that a range of moisture contents is obtained which includes the optimum moisture. In general, increments of 1 to 2% are suitable for sandy and gravelly soils and of 2 to 4% for cohesive soils. To increase the accuracy of the test, it is advisable to reduce the increments of water in the region of the optimum moisture content.

6.1.4 Calculation

1. Bulk density, D in g/cm^3 of each compacted specimen is calculated from the following equation.

   D = (W2-W1)/Vm

   Where,

   W1 = Weight in g of mould + base plate

   W2 = Weight in g of mould + base plate + soil

   Vm = Volume of mould, i.e. 1000 cm^3

6.1.5 Graph

The dry density, γd, obtained in a series of determinations is plotted against the corresponding moisture content 'M'. A smooth curve is then drawn through the resulting points and the position of the maximum on this curve is determined, which is called maximum dry density (M.D.D). And the corresponding moisture content is called optimum moisture content

(O.M.C.). Plot of dry Unit Weight v/s Moisture Content (Compaction Curve)

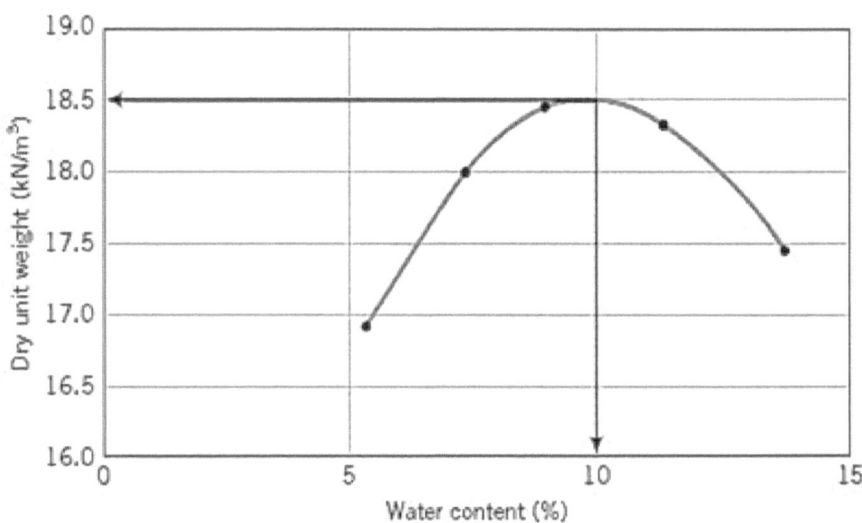

In this case, the dry unit weight/density is 18.5 KN/cubic meter and OMC is 10%

6.1.6 Execution

At the time of construction of high banks and roads, soil is spread in about eight-inch layers. Water of measured quantity at OMC minus water present in soil is sprinkled by water tankers and then rolled with heavy road rollers for full compaction. Very less water content would not give desired results after rolling. Water works as a facilitator to bring soil particles together to produce a compact soil mass.

Thickness of the layer to be compacted depends on the size of the roller. Before permitting the spread of the next layer, lab tests are carried on the freshly-rolled surface to ensure proper compaction of soil. Normally, the roller should start working on the surface without leaving any marks for good compaction. Even if a person walks and tries to press it with his shoe's heel, it should not leave any impression on the freshly-compacted surface.

In small trenches and foundations, soil compaction is done by plate compactors and hand-held rammers.

6.1.7 Field tests

First, soil is tested in borrow area for moisture content. About 2 kg of soil as in borrow area is weighed (W1). It is heated on a stove and again weighed (W2).

Moisture content is (W1-W2) × 100/W1= W3%

Water to be added while compaction = OMC-W3 per cubic meter.

Further corrections are made if it is hot sun or slightly raining for loss/ addition of water while working.

Work is stopped in case of heavy rains and the area under construction is covered by trampolines.

On visual inspection, if it is felt that the compaction is completed by the rollers, a few samples are collected by digging small pits in the area and the soil recovered is weighed. The pit is filled with measured dry sand and the volume of sand needed is measured. Field density is equal to the weight of the earth excavated from the pit divided by the volume of sand used to fill the pit. Generally, 85% to 95% of dry density at OMC is acceptable. Soil becomes more compact with load of further layers, but in top layers, maximum possible density is tried.

6.1.8 Difficult soil and weather conditions

On one of the major high bank projects, with bank height of 40 meters, OMC could not be maintained due to continuous rains and the soil used was over-saturated. It was spread and continuously compacted by the movement of heavy trucks and bulldozers since there was no other alternative. It was felt that with the heavy load of the bank, the soil would be compacted to its maximum extent with time and load.

This theory did work and the soil was sufficiently compacted but the water released from soil did not find any escape route and created heavy pressure within the soil mass, resulting in landslides on both sides of the bank after completion of the work.

It would be better in such cases if vertical stone columns or horizontal sand drains are added at suitable intervals for the release of trapped water through these columns/drains.

On a steel plant in Hazira, Gujarat, the ground surface had a thick layer of dune sand having very low liquid limit and similar sand was available as fill material. Deep pile foundations were built for all structures. For roads, Sand Vicks were used. Stockyards for iron ore and finished products—stone columns measuring 450 mm in diameter and 12 meters deep were added to stockpile areas. These Sand Vicks and stone columns not only helped in draining of water due to compaction but also acted as reinforcement adding to the load-bearing capacity of the bank/road surface. No problems arose; it has been time-tested.

Stone columns are built by driving a casing with a bottom closed by a cast-in-situ piling rig, fill the casing with uniform-sized stones and remove the casing.

Sand Vicks are made with thick cloth stitched like a 2-inch diameter pipe, filled with clean coarse sand and dropped in a 3-inch diameter hole made by driving a pipe in the ground using a tripod and hammer.

Engineers have to find solutions to difficult problems in any adverse conditions with their experience and innovation.

For difficult soils, 5 to 12% sand or 2 to 5% cement is mixed thoroughly while spreading on the bank for improving load-bearing capacities. Specially-designed mixing trucks are available for this purpose.

6.2 Sand

Sand is generally found in rivers, in different grades and grain-size thickness depending upon the distance of the source from the hills where the river originates.

Sand is formed by the rubbing of stones coming down the hills due to the turbulent flow of water in rivers and settling down in the river beds as water speed is reduced. Upstream of the river, small boulders and pebbles settle down on river beds and slowly, their particle-grain size is further reduced as the river moves further. As the river flows further, these stone pieces become smaller, clay particles flowing with sand and settle on the river bed with even smaller sand particles called **silt.** Silt is a mixture of fine sand and clay in small particles, generally having high clay content.

Sand used for construction should be free of silt and clay and if traces are found, the sand should be washed and screened to remove silt and clay before use in construction.

Sand is used for making cement-sand mortar for filling in joints of brick-laying, plastering and is mixed with bigger stone pieces called aggregates and cement for making concrete.

For roads and high banks, sand is used as filter layers between layers of earth and big stones.

Sand is also mixed with soils of poor quality in small proportions—say, 5%—to improve structural quality of such soils on construction projects. Poor quality of soils with high fines content, arrest water within their body and create weak pockets of water which reduce the soil's load-bearing capacity. The addition of sand mixed with soil avoids formation of water pockets and provides better flow of water, increasing the load-bearing capacity of the soil. This is called *sand dozing* to soils.

6.3 Aggregates/stone chips

Stone chips, called coarse aggregates, are produced by crushing stone in stone crushers to the specified sizes as per requirements of the engineers for different uses in construction. In hilly terrain, aggregates are produced by blasting rocky hills to break rock into big boulders. These rock boulders are transported to crushing plants for further processing and then dispatched to project sites.

Rock is also found in the form of big round and oval pieces in rivers on foothills. These are called boulders, while smaller pieces, called pebbles, are also used as concrete aggregates provided they qualify in the quality and size criteria.

Rock is available in different qualities according to their natural process of formation. Only specific, good rock is used for producing aggregates.

Stone is used in different sizes in the construction of ports, harbour, roads and all types of structures.

Rock formed by volcanic eruption hundreds of years ago is called igneous rock; it is the best for construction. Igneous rock is generally black in colour, homogeneous, heavy, free of organic impurities and non-abrasive. However, in absence of igneous rock, other types of rock are also used for construction, with some restrictions.

6.4 Processing of rock for construction

Rock is first quarried from mountainous quarries by chiselling or blasting. Blasted rock pieces are further reduced to small pieces by secondary blasting by putting a small piece of explosive in big boulders. Blasted rock of not more than 12 inches size are loaded in trucks and taken to a crusher.

Big crushers have a primary crusher to break big pieces into small pieces and, in the process; some rock is also broken in even smaller pieces, as desired. Whole, crushed material is passed through a vibrating screen which segregates material according to the sizes required and shifted to separate heaps—with the help of conveyors—for loading and transport to actual users. Bigger rock pieces are shifted from the vibratory screen by a conveyor to a secondary crusher for further crushing, screening and segregating.

Smaller crushing units do not have primary crushers and hence, the feed to crusher is restricted to 6 to 8 inches according to crusher design.

6.5 Expensive varieties of rock

Expensive varieties of rock include coal (diamond is also rock; it is a crystal form of coal), gold ore, marble, building stones, limestone, iron ore and many minerals.

Gold, silver, copper, platinum, iron and other minerals are found on big hills and underground, mixed with earth, with 40% to 85% metal content. Coal found in big hills covered by about one meter of earth and directly excavated is good for use. The picture below is an open cast gold mine.

Kolar gold field mines in India

Gold ore is taken to smelting plants; it is heated in closed furnaces to the melting point. Metal, in the liquid form, gets settled at the bottom and the sludge, containing mostly clay, is removed from top. This liquid metal is moulded in the form of bricks and sent to designated refineries for further processing and separating of all the metals. Bricks from smelting plants contain a mix of all the metals like gold, silver copper and other metals with metal content of 80 to 85%. Up to the smelting stage, the process is simple and could be done even at home.

Mining of minerals with less than 40% metal content is generally not economical.

Mining of rock for construction and minerals is a big business worldwide and could be deliberated as a subject by itself, in areas of interest/opportunities.

6.6 Lime

Lime is the oldest binding material used with stones and bricks in the construction industry. Still, it is used in abundance for various applications.

Lime—mainly calcium carbonates—is found in abundance in many parts of the country and it is recovered by excavation and chiselling from hills and crushed into small pieces.

These pieces can be directly used after soaking in water for a few hours and filtered through a strainer. Lime mixed with water is passed freely through the strainer and impurities like mud and stones are left on the strainer; they are to be thrown away. After drying, it becomes semi-solid and can be preserved in bags for use. This is called **slake lime**.

Alternatively, lime is burnt in kilns and ground into a fine powder. This is packed in air-tight bags and sold in the market. This is called **quick lime.**

Lime is used for whitewashing of buildings, as mortar when mixed with sand for plaster and buildings walls and joining bricks in brick walls.

Lime is the main ingredient of cement.

Lime is also mixed with cement for producing concrete and other applications.

Lime is a good disinfectant and it is spread in drains and roadsides for better hygiene.

As stated earlier, it is used as dozing material in earthwork.

6.7 Cement

Cement is a well-known commodity used for construction. Cement is produced by burning limestone in furnaces and then fine-grinding its well-burnt small pieces, called clinker. Sand, clay, gypsum and iron ore are added in small proportions at different stages of manufacturing. The percentage of these and other additives decide the quality parameters of cement for different applications. The extent of fine-grinding and the presence of disodium silicate and tri-sodium silicate in cement decide its strength-gaining properties when mixed with water. The finer the grinding, the stronger the cement will be.

Cement is available in different grades and applications as per one's requirement. It is a perishable item and gets spoilt when it comes in contact with moisture. Hence, one must be careful in ensuring its storage requirements are met. It must be stored on dry wooden pallets in free-of-moisture containers. Even then, the maximum shelf life is usually 45 days from the date of manufacture. First-come should be used first.

6.8 Steel in different forms

Iron is produced by burning iron ore in different processes at about 1400 degree centigrade in the presence of oxygen and coal/natural gas. The iron in the different types of oxides turns into liquid iron and carbon dioxide is released into the atmosphere. Clay and other impurities float on molten iron and are taken away by mechanical processes from the furnace. This is called pig iron, sponge iron, etc. as per the process of manufacture.

This iron is again heated in another furnace and nickel, cobalt, carbon and other substances are mixed according to the requirement and the quality of steel being produced. Steel is produced in liquid form in its furnace and is melded in different forms for further processing as per requirements—like bars, plates, channels, angles and other shapes, in different sizes. Galvanized steel is produced by dipping finished steel pieces in a container filled with molten zinc. This gives a layer of zinc on steel uniformly.

Steel is also produced in smaller sections by melting waste cut-pieces of used steel in construction. Mouldings by this process are called ingots and those obtained directly from iron with proper mixing of additives are called billets.

Steel produced by ingots is cheaper to billet's steel since it does not have the same quality parameters as steel produced from billets.

Steel for construction is available in the market in different grades and qualities with a wide variation in prices. Hence, purchases should be as per specifications provided in the contract supported by laboratory tests.

Care should be taken for accuracy in its dimensions. Generally, 2% variation in size is allowed. Hence, steel is sold in lengths if its weight is less than the standard weight. After some time, mill rollers get worn out, resulting in a heavier product. This heavier steel is sold by weight—a loss to the contractor. For large quantities, it is preferred to take sample weights at site and compare with the standard weights given in the books and pay the supplier accordingly.

6.9 Timber

Timber has many applications in the construction industry. Raw timber is used in construction for providing temporary and permanent supports like beams, columns, struts, scantlings, shuttering and melds for concrete as per the shapes of the concrete structure required to be constructed. Timber is cut in standard sizes in sawmills and sold to contractors as per their requirements.

Broadly, there are two types of timber—soft wood is used for non-load bearing applications and hard wood for load-bearing applications. Care should be taken that columns and beams are free of knots. Knots break faster when subjected to loads.

6.9.1 Timber for industrial use

Timber has always been used extensively for construction of buildings, industrial sheds and other structure of permanent nature. Until recently, say, 60 to 75 years ago, good quality timber like Teak (south-east Asia), Cedar (from Lebanon), Pine (Europe), Shisham, Sal, Rose and many more others were available in India for building houses, furniture and other applications by cutting, dressing and melding timber cut from these trees. These products used to be very beautiful and durable. Woodwork made from these in temples, churches and other historical places are still intact and look beautiful after standing for more than a century.

Now, due to restrictions on deforestation and the shortage of good quality timber, timber is used as it is available.

Timber wastes are mechanically processed and are available in the market for building construction and industrial use. These products are good and are proving to be a satisfactory replacement to original timber. However, the quality differs from manufacturer to manufacturer.

6.9.2 Different types of processed timber for industrial use

The following are the different forms of processed timber:

- Veneers

- Plywood

- Fibber boards

- Impreg timbers

- Compreg timbers

- Hard boards

- Glulam

- Chip board

- Block board

- Flush door shutters

Veneers

Veneers are nothing but thin layers of quality wood like teak, pine etc. These are obtained by cutting the wood with a sharp knife in a rotary cutter.

In a rotary cutter, the wood log is rotated against the sharp knife or saw and cuts it into thin sheets. These thin sheets are dried in kilns and, finally, veneers are obtained.

Veneers are used to manufacture different wood products like plywood, block boards etc. and are glued to the top surface for giving good appearance, finish and durability.

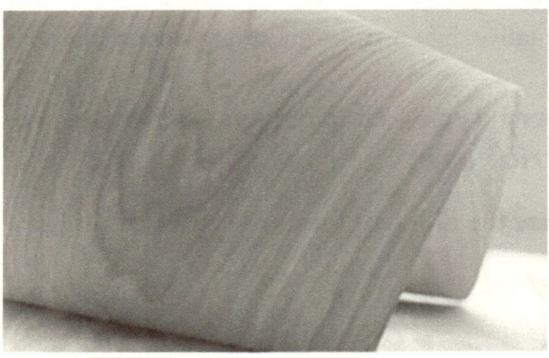

Plywood

Ply means thin. Plywood is a board obtained by adding thin layers of wood or veneers one above the other. The joining of successive layers is done by suitable adhesives.

The layers are glued and pressed with some form of pressure—either in hot or cold conditions. In hot conditions, a 150 to 200°C temperature is maintained and a hydraulic press is used to press the layers. In cold conditions, room temperature is maintained and 0.7 to 1.4 N/mm² pressure is applied.

Plywood has so many uses. It is used for doors, partition walls, ceilings, panelling walls, formwork for concrete, etc.

Due to its decorative appearance, it is used for buildings like theatres, auditoriums, temples, churches, restaurants, etc. in architectural purpose.

Plywood having teak veneer on one face is called teak plywood or teak-veneered ply-wood.

Fibber boards

Fibber boards are made of wood fibbers, vegetable fibbers, etc. They are rigid boards and are called as reconstructed wood.

The collected fibbers are boiled in hot water and then transferred into a closed vessel. Steam, under a low pressure, is pumped into the vessel and the pressure increased suddenly.

Due to the sudden increment of pressure, the wood fibbers explode and the natural adhesive gets separated from the fibbers. Then, they are cleaned and spread on a wire screen in the form of loose sheets. This matter is pressed in between steel plates and finally, fibber boards are obtained.

Fibber boards are used for several purposes in the construction industry, such as for wall panelling, ceilings, partitions, flush doors, flooring material, etc. They are also used as sound-insulating material.

Impreg Timbers

Impreg timber is a timber covered fully or partly with resin. Thin layers of wood or veneers are taken and dipped in resin solution. The resin solution fills up the voids in the wood and a consolidated mass occurs. Then, it is heated at 150 to 160°C and, finally, Impreg timber develops. This is available in the market under different names such as sun gloss, sun mica, Formica, etc.

Impreg timber has good resistance against moisture, weathering, acids and electricity. It is strong, durable and provides a beautiful appearance. It is used for making wood melds, furniture, decorative products, etc.

Compreg Timbers

It is similar to Impreg timber but in this case, the timber is cured under pressure conditions. So, it is more strengthened than Impreg timber. Its specific gravity lies from 1.30 to 1.35.

Hardboards

Hardboard is usually 3 mm thick and made from wood pulp. Wood pulp is compressed with some pressure and made into solid boards. The top surface of the board is smooth and hard, while the bottom surface is rough. Hardboards are generally classified into three types as follows:

Types	Density (kg/m³)	Available thickness (mm)
Medium	480–800	6, 8, 10, 12
Normal	800–1200	3, 4, 5, 6, 9, 12
Tempered	>1200	3, 4, 5, 6, 9, 12

Glulam

Glulam means glued and laminated wood. Solid wood veneers are glued to form sheets and then are laminated with suitable resins.

This type of sheet is very much suitable in the construction of chemical factories, long-span roofs in sports stadiums, indoor swimming pools, etc. Curved wooden structures can also be constructed using Glulam sheets.

Chipboard

Chipboards are another type of industrial timber which is made of wood particles, rice husk ash or bagasse. These are dissolved in resins for some time and then heated. After that, it is pressed with some pressure and boards are made. These are also called particle boards.

Block board

Block board is a board containing a core made of wood strips. The wood strips are generally obtained from the leftovers of solid timber conversion, etc. These strips are glued and made into a solid form.

Veneers are used as faces to cover this solid core. The width of the core should not exceed 25 mm. If the width of the core is less than 7 mm, then it is called a lamination board.

Block boards are generally used for partitions, panelling, marine and river crafts, railway carriages, etc.

Flush Door Shutters

Flush door shutters made in factories are widely used nowadays. They are generally available in 25 mm, 30 mm or 35 mm thicknesses. Factory-made flush board shutters are of different types such as cellular core, hollow core, block board core, etc.

07

Concrete

Concrete is a mixture of cement, stone pieces, sand and water, mixed together thoroughly by any method, in a semi-liquid form. When placed in a mould and left to dry, it takes the shape of the mould and becomes solid in a few hours. Generally, it should be poured and settled in a mould within 45 minutes of mixing water with cement. It gains strength slowly and becomes strong in about 30 days. Concrete is durable and widely used in construction for building various structures of all types.

In the mixture of stone pieces and sand, there are bound to be tiny air pockets all around. The size and quantity of these pockets depends upon the selection of different sizes of stone particles and sand, and their mix. Big stone pieces have bigger pockets and smaller pieces go and get accommodated in this big pocket. Thus, smaller and smaller pieces get adjusted in these pockets called voids. When cement and water mixed in the form of a thin paste is added to this mass, the paste goes around all the particles and fills up remaining voids. The concrete mix is also shaken by vibrators to facilitate this paste going to a maximum-possible number of voids and filling them up. Soon, this paste, through a chemical reaction, becomes solid and strong, thereby making all the concrete masses strong structures.

Concrete for all the structures is the same but its strength varies based on composition of its ingredients and their quality.

Concrete is strong in compression and shear loads but weak in tension. Steel bars are used and embedded in concrete to take care of tension loads and to increase other load-bearing characteristics as required.

7.1 Concrete mix design

As stated earlier, cement concrete is produced by mixing cement, aggregates and water. Aggregates are inert material in small pieces. There are gaps between these pieces in a heap which are known as voids. Take a measured volume of aggregates in a container and make sure that it is well packed. If the water is added in a measured quantity, it will fill up the voids and replace the air before appearing on the top of the fill of aggregates in the container. It will not increase the volume. The quantity of this water that fills in the voids is the total quantity of air voids replaced by it. Mix half the voids by aggregates smaller to the size of voids and shake the container. These pieces will fill in the voids without increasing the total volume of the container. However, some water that has been replaced by the stones will come out. It should be removed and measured. The volume of this water should be the same as the volume of the smaller aggregates that are added. This exercise is repeated a few times i.e., adding smaller particles of aggregates—say, about 50%—of the remaining voids, till the particles in the smallest size are added, including the sand, without increasing the volume of the container. This volume of stones in the container will ultimately contain the maximum quantity of stones and the least volume of air or water voids.

This mass of aggregates is a mix of stones of different sizes and grades. So, it is termed as graded volume of aggregates. While doing this exercise, if a few excess pieces remain on top after shaking the container, they should be removed and measured.

Simpler methods are provided in books of mix design to achieve the best-graded combination of different sizes of aggregates including fine aggregates. This was only an illustration for understanding.

Water and cement are mixed in a defined ratio known as water to cement ratio. A table of water to cement ratio for different strengths of concrete is available with the supplier of the cement. The lesser the content of water in the water to cement ratio, the higher is the strength of the concrete. The lesser quantity of the voids, the lesser is the volume of the water-cement paste. Hence, there is less cement consumption.

This paste is poured into the container and shaken well and measured. Cement used in the paste to fill all the voids is the quantity needed for this concrete and the quantity of cement used is the requirement for the volume of concrete in the container.

Thus, the lesser the volume of free voids in graded aggregates, the lesser the paste is required. Thus, the better the grading of aggregates, less water and more strength is achieved for the same quantity of cement. A typical concrete-mixing plant is shown below. There are big, vertical silos for cement storage and a circular drum for concrete mixing. These are fed cement by screw conveyors. Aggregates are fed from behind in different sizes. The truck with a round drum on the back is the concrete truck mixer. It is used to carry concrete from the plant to the site. This truck is known as a transit mixer and the concrete is continuously agitated by the rotation of the drum to avoid hardening in transit.

7.1.1 Workability

One of the more important factors is the workability of concrete. Concrete should not be too harsh or too wet to handle. The workability requirements are defined in the design of the structure and are generally measured as slump. There is a conical cylinder of a defined size open from both sides, known as a slump cone. Keep the slump cone vertical on a flat steel plate with the wider area at the bottom. Fill up the slump cone with wet concrete in three portions. Each time, tap the concrete twenty times with a tamping rod. Once the slump cone is filled up to the brim, smoothen the top with a trowel and discard the excess concrete. Lift the cone gently and a heap of concrete in the cone, as it comes out, will go down and collapse a little. This level difference is measured and is termed as a slump. Now, make a few test samples with different cement/aggregate/water ratios and slumps in the form of cubes or cylinders. Test these cubes/cylinders in a crushing machine after three days, seven days and twenty-eight days to obtain the crushing strength of the concrete in the field laboratory and finalize the single mix which gives it the heaviest unit weight, reasonable slump and the greatest strength. A few sample tests cubes or cylinders are always kept in spare for fifty-two days. Tests should always be done and in case test results are not as good as expected, test cubes and cylinders are kept wet. They are submerged in water and taken out of the water about an hour before the test, to be reasonably dry at the time of a crushing test.

7.1.2 Other parameters

Besides the water to cement ratio, concrete strength depends on the breaking or the crushing strength of the weakest set of particles in the concrete, under the load. These weak particles would break before the cement bond breaks. Thus, the quality of aggregates is equally important. On a road project, the maximum crushing strength of concrete is attained in a laboratory test was 300 kgs per square centimetre due to constraints in the quality of aggregates. So, bridges and culvert structures were designed as Reinforced Cement Concrete (RCC) structures instead of pre-stressed concrete structures needing a minimum of 600 kgs per square centimetre crushing strength.

Cement paste spreads around aggregates and glues them together. Hence, it is dependent on the total surface area of the aggregates available. If silt, which is very fine, having a large surface area or too much fine sand, is mixed in the concrete, the surface area will increase, resulting in weak concrete. Silt is so fine that sometimes, cement does not reach all around all the particles, leaving loose pockets in concrete which is dangerous and makes the concrete weak.

Many times, aggregates are rejected and ordered to be sourced from long distances at extra time and costs to the project knowingly or unknowingly, instead of washing and screening aggregates and sand for the removal of excessive silt and traces of clay present in them. Aggregates and sand must be washed thoroughly before use and such rejection can be avoided. This exercise requires some additional equipment and manpower at additional costs to the contractor but is always cheaper than sourcing this material from long distances and saving in cement consumption.

7.2 Concrete has different names depending upon the method of construction and nature of the structure it is intended to be used for

7.2.1 Reinforced Cement Concrete (RCC)

RCC is the most common and safe kind of concrete structures since they are easy to build with the least chances of failure. Depending upon the quality parameters used in construction, an adequate factor of safety is provided in the design of these structures. The basic design consideration is that concrete is good in taking compressive loads and some shear loads. Tensile and shear strength to the structure are provided by re-bars placed at locations of tensile and shear stress in the structure. Compressive strength is provided by the concrete. Sometimes, if compressive loads are more than the capacity of the concrete, re-bars are also provided in compression zones to support the concrete in these areas.

- Detailed construction drawings are provided by the design engineer with shapes and sizes of all members of the concrete structure.

- The design engineer specifies the strength of the concrete and re-bars that are to be used.

- Accordingly, procurement actions are taken for re-bars and concrete. Rebars must be tested to confirm specifications while procuring. There are vast differences in the quality and prices of re-bars available in the market.

- Formwork, better known as shuttering, are the molds made out of steel or timber or a combination of both. Concrete is poured in these molds and it takes the shape of the structure after becoming solid.

- These molds are assembled by bolts and nuts and removed carefully after the concrete has gained enough strength. Normally, vertical sides are removed after 8 to 12 hours, bottoms of slabs after 5 to 7 days and beam bottoms after 21 days of pouring concrete in forms. The decision to remove the shuttering for slabs and beam bottoms are done by testing concrete samples taken at the time of pouring the concrete.

- Scaffolding is the support framework made of steel or timber or a combination of both, on which the concrete formwork is fitted and they are strong enough to take loads of concrete and workers moving around for doing the work.

- Formwork and scaffoldings are designed carefully for strength and ease of working. In case of repetitive use of formwork for over 15 times, steel formwork is fabricated and used.

- Timber forms with a plywood face are used when the usage is limited to seven to ten times. Sometimes, plywood bolted on a steel frame is also used and give results better than steel straight forms.

- Cutting and bending of reinforcement bars are planned by preparing bar-bending schedules from the drawing and properly checked for any mistakes. Efficient bar-bending schedules will have minimum wastages. A bar-bending schedule is a drawing or statement of how the re-bars are to be bent and fixed in the formwork with all dimensions, sizes and numbers.

- Re-bars are cut and bent with proper identification tags, and are brought to the site on schedule.

- All the above activities have to be done simultaneously through micro-planning. These re-bars bent in proper shapes and sizes including epoxy paint, if required, should be ready before the site is ready to accept them for use and continue to be available in stages according to the work schedule.

- The first survey is carried out and the location of the concrete member is marked on the existing structure or ground as the case may be. Scaffolding is fixed as per the design at the location. On this scaffolding, the bottom of the beam or slab is fixed. One side of the beam is also fixed.

- On this bottom of the beam, re-bars are fixed in proper shapes and sizes as per the drawing and bar-bending schedule, supported against the vertical formwork fixed on one side to avoid bending or falling down.

- Cover blocks of cement mortar or plastic are provided on all sides.

- Once ready, the forms and re-bars are checked, including shapes and levels. The forms are cleaned again and then closed with proper supports.

- Now, concrete is poured in the forms.

- While pouring concrete, it is extensively shaken by equipment called vibrators so that it flows and reaches all the corners of the formwork and is uniformly distributed. Concrete is produced free of any air pockets or honeycombs.

- Honeycomb is a loose pocket in the concrete structure, with or without some cement paste, to be removed, treated and repaired. This has to be avoided and an excess of honeycombs could made the structure liable to be rejected.

- Care has to be taken to ensure that the top re-bars placed in beams and slabs do not collapse or distort by the movement of workers and while pouring concrete. This will reduce the strength of the re-bars available to the structure.

- Similarly, minimum cover to concrete, i.e. distance of rebars from the formwork's surface has to be maintained for all the bars placed along the formwork to avoid corrosion of steel and losing strength with time. The cover is kept between 15 mm to 75 mm depending upon the exposure of the structure to chemicals and the weather conditions.

Vibrators are available in the following types

- Needle vibrators are 25 mm to 60 mm in diameter. They are small cylinders about 300 to 600 mm long with an eccentric rod fitted into two end bearings. When this rod rotates, the cylinder vibrates. These rods are connected to a motor with a flexible cable in a rubber hose pipe about two meters long. When this vibrator is immersed in wet concrete, the concrete shakes, gets spread in the whole formwork and gets compacted.

- Form vibrators are bolted from outside to forms. When operated, the whole formwork vibrates and the concrete is spread all over inside the form and around steel re-bars.

Curing of concrete

As the concrete surface starts becoming hard, heat is generated in the concrete due to chemical action of cement with water. If this heat is not neutralised by cooling, it will increase the temperature of the fresh concrete and water vapor will be generated. This vapor, under pressure, could damage the concrete by creating small cracks to escape out of the concrete mass. Water is sprinkled to keep it cool and avoid cracking due to heating and formation of water vapors. This is more important when high grades of cement are used since, in such cases, the heat generated is much higher. The normal curing time is 21 days after pouring of the concrete.

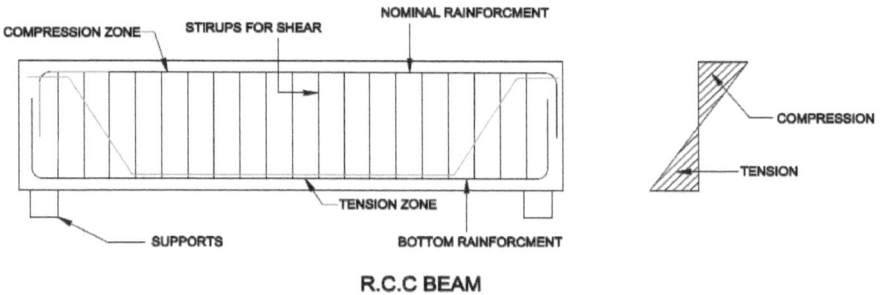

R.C.C BEAM

7.2.2 Pre-stressed concrete

If we try to bend a small, green branch of a plant while holding its two ends with two hands, it can be noticed that on one side, small tissues of the branch come closer and on the other side, they move apart in the bending zone. On one side, tissues move closer since they are compressed (called the **compression zone**) and on the other side, they are pulled apart (called the

tension zone). In the compression zone, the length of the branch reduces and it increases in the tension zone due to pushing and pulling of tissues. It is difficult to measure but by looking carefully, one can see it. Concrete is a mix of stone aggregates glued together with cement. If one tries to pull it, the bond of cement would soon break. But if compressed, it will provide resistance and crumble on excessive load. Hence, concrete is **week in tension** load applications due to pulling and **strong in compression** loads applied by pushing between two ends.

Steel rods also have the similar characteristics but they are stronger than concrete. By any process, if one can compress the tension zone of concrete before a load is applied, on application of the tension load, first the compressive load would be neutralized by the tension load and the structure would go in tension stress mode **only** after neutralization of induced compressive loads entirely.

In **pre-stressed concrete technology,** the concrete member is compressed in its tension zone before applying the load. On load application, induced tension would neutralize the compressive load first till the end of the induced compression and then, the concrete would be required to face tensile loads.

Induced compressive stresses are substantive and even on full loads; the structure would still have some compressive stresses in balance in this pre-stressed portion of the structure. Hence, this part of the concrete of the structure would never be subjected to tensile stresses and the property of good compressive strength of the concrete is utilized to maximum possibility. Obviously, the concrete's quality has to be consistent and with very high compressive strengths.

Compressive stress is induced by providing a bunch of special high-tensile steel wires in a designed profile before concreting. After the concrete is properly cured and has gained strength, these wires are pulled to induce compressive stress in the surrounding concrete and are locked. These compressive strengths are introduced in concrete in the following steps for a pre-stressed beam:

- First formwork for the bottom and one side of the beam are fixed in place.

- Pre-stressing cables are prepared according to the specifications and sizes provided in the drawings.

- Re-bars as per the drawings are fixed on the formwork. These bars are for extra support, to cover contingencies including handling stresses and shear forces.

- Pre-stressing cables are fixed in the beam in a parabolic shape. The bending moment of a simple, supported beam is the highest in the centre of the beam and reduces to zero in a parabolic order as one moves to end support. Hence, these cables are to be placed in designed parabolic profiles without any kinks or other mistakes. For convenience of fixing cables, their profile is marked on the formwork and cables are fixed as per these profiles marked and tied to re-bars.

- These cables come in a thin, flexible metal casing called sheeting. Care has to be taken to ensure that these casings are watertight and are not damaged in handling.

- Both the ends of each pre-stressing cable are fitted with a female cone. This cone is a circular, hollow cylinder of concrete, about 250 mm in diameter and 200 mm in length, with a corrugated, tapered hole in the cylinder. This cone is fitted on the formwork with a matching hole to the hole in the cone. High-tensile cables are passed through this hole. At least one meter of cable wires should be out of forms on both sides of the cable.

- After checking that all the cables and re-bars are properly placed, the formwork is closed and made ready for concreting.

- Concrete is poured in the forms carefully and it is to be made sure that it reaches all the corners of the formwork including the cables. For proper distribution of concrete and its compaction, form vibrators are preferred. Needle vibrators may damage the sheeting of cables and being a thin structure, the concrete may not reach everywhere.

- In spite of taking all the care, the sheeting of cables can get damaged somewhere and cement grout could have entered into the cables and created a bond. After a few hours of concreting, these cables are hammered gently to break any obstruction in them.

- Concrete would need about ten days to achieve the minimum strength required for pre-stressing. Start pre-stressing only after sufficient strength is reached; this should be confirmed by laboratory tests.

- Clean the pre-stressing wires properly and, again, check by hammering that they are kept loose in the beam's cables and insert the male cone loosely fitting into the female cone, keeping wires evenly distributed in the groves provided between the two cones.

- Fix pre-stressing jacks to the pre-stressing wires on both sides of the cables.

- Pull the cables from both ends using the jacks and provide required tension equally on both sides. Check elongation of the wires. Elongation is checked by putting a mark on one or two wires before beginning pre-stressing. Check the distance of this mark before and after tensioning from the face of the concrete.

- After pre-tensioning is completed, push the male cone hard into the female cone with a piston in the pre-stressing jack and make it tight-fitted.

- Release the jacks and repeat the process for the other cables as instructed.

- After a few days, check for any slippages in wires. If there is any slippage, break the male cone and repeat the pre-stressing of that cable.

- It would be noticed that the beam lifts by a few centimetres in its centre; this upward deflection is measured and checked with expectations as per design.

- Grout the cables with a non-shrink grout for pre-stressing wires to be in the integral part of the beam and to remain protected from corrosion.

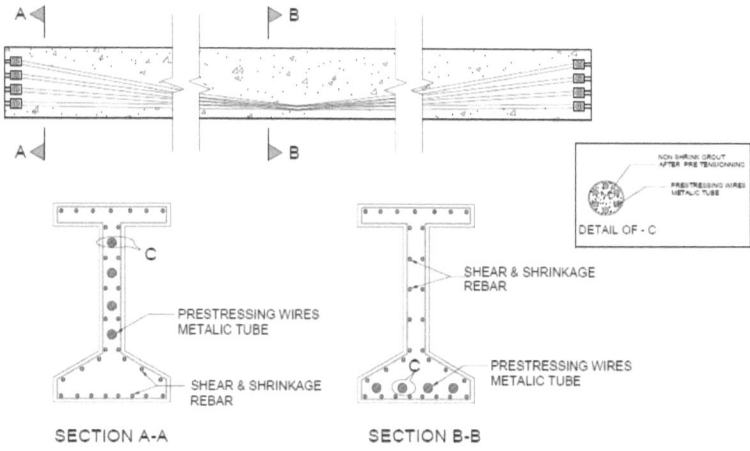

With this, pre-stressing is completed. This is as per the Freyssinet system of pre-stressing of concrete. Many more systems are available at the choice of designers but the concepts are the same.

In some cases, pre-stressing is done in multiple stages. In the first stage, enough compression loads in the concrete are provided in beams to neutralize tension to be created in the beam due to own weight and handling loads until they are placed in their final location. In the process, tensile loads created due to weight of the beam, called dead load, nullify a majority of the pre-stressed compressive strength. Now, a few more cables are pre-stressed to take care of live loads. This is marvellous but concrete has to be of very good quality to take multiple stress reversals. Pre-stressed concrete in beams and other structure is preferred to RCC since it is almost half the weight, easier to handle and cheaper in construction.

7.2.3 Roller-compacted concrete

Major dam projects have a wide base that slowly tapers and reduces in width as it goes up in the designed shape of a huge mass. These masses are built to provide a big, thick wall, stable with its gravity to resist the pressure of water on one side of the wall and the other side remaining free. These dams are built using earth fill, rock fill or concrete. In most cases, earth, as well as rock, is locally available. Some rock also comes out of the excavation and is used for the project in some form or the other.

In normal concrete for structures, cement consumption is more than 10% of total concrete weight with 75 mm being maximum size of aggregates and elaborate infrastructure and construction procedures are needed.

With the recently developed roller-compacted concrete technology, graded aggregates in 150 mm or 100 mm down in sizes are mixed with 3 to 5% cement and added with very little water as per designed water-cement ratio confirming to concrete strength requirements. The mix is almost dry but no voids should be there after compaction as confirmed by laboratory tests. This aggregate, cement and water mix is spread by trucks and motor graders in layers of 300 to 400 mm across the dam section and rolled by heavy rollers for a few minutes and rolling is completed before the initial setting of cement concrete. This is very fast as compared to regular concrete and earthwork construction. Cement content is less than half or one-third of regular concrete of similar properties and the working procedure is less than one-third time-taking compared to earthwork. The section of the dam is also very small compared to earthen dam. This technology is evolving fast and will soon be used in the construction of very heavy and mass concrete structures.

This technology is better than cement concrete due to the various benefits stated above and no precautions/damages are probable from the excessive generation of heat due to hydration, etc.

Explanations

- **Strength of the concrete depends upon the strength of the sand-cement mortar**

  Mortar should be little more than sufficient to fill all the voids

- **The bigger the size of graded aggregate, lesser the surface area and volume of voids for a given volume. Hence, lesser cement paste/content will be used for larger-sized aggregates.**

  Very little of a thick paste is required for a nearly-dry mix for roller compacted concrete compared to wet concrete with a high slump in the case of regular concrete.

- **Hence, overall, just almost one-fourth to one-third cement is required for roller compacted concrete compared to normal concrete.**

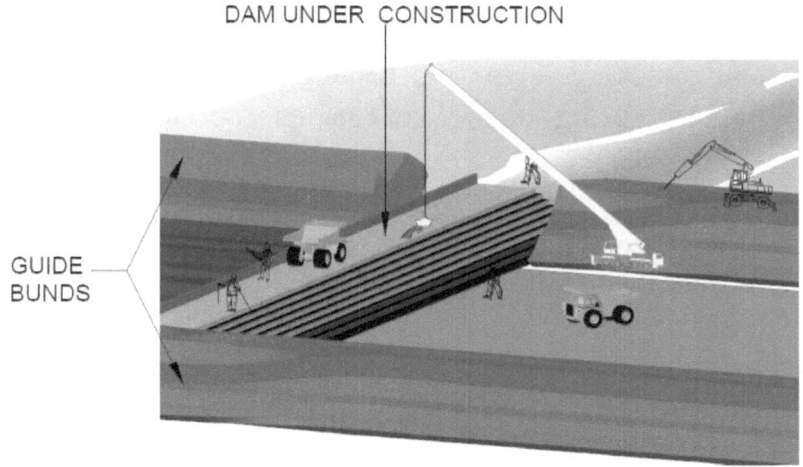

Roller-compacted concreting on a dam site in progress

7.2.4 Plum concrete

In some mass concrete foundations, boulders of say 150 mm size up to 30% of the total quantity of concrete are mixed into the wet concrete. This adds to the economics and saves from heat generation. Such concretes are called plum concretes. After at least two layers of wet concrete is completed, well-shaped and thoroughly washed, angular rock pieces with a maximum size of not more than 60% of the layer of pour thickness are placed in the concrete, keeping a distance of more than one-and-a-half times of the biggest size of the aggregates in the concrete. The bottom of the boulders should be embedded in the wet concrete to avoid voids at the bottom. Concreting is continued without stopping. These rock pieces become an integral part of the concrete structure.

Plum concrete is not advisable in reinforced cement concrete subjected to heavy bending and shear loads. **In pre-stressed concrete, plum concrete is totally not acceptable.**

Advantages

- **Cost savings as some part of the concrete is replaced by much cheaper boulders.**

- **Cost-saving due to lesser involvement of concrete production and conveying equipment. Labour cost is slightly higher for boulder-placing compared to concrete pouring.**

- **Total operation time gets reduced.**

- **Heat generation in concrete is substantially reduced, hence it is technically preferred.**

7.2.5 Colcrete–underwater concreting for large foundations

Colcrete is a method used for concreting a thick block in a confined area in deep, underwater conditions. Colcrete is a process of concreting by injecting high-pressure cement-water or cement-water-sand grout in voids of a big container filled with loose aggregates or stones deep underwater. This grout is fed in highly-agitated conditions and **does not allow chemical action between cement and water till the agitation is reduced or stopped**. In the agitated state, all fine solids mixed with water remain in a colloidal state and do not react with each other—nor get segregated—until settled in the container. Since the concreting is done in a colloidal state, it is called **colcrete**. It is mainly used in concreting plug of deep well foundations and foundations of marine structures.

Iron ore in its powder form is transported hundreds of kilometres in a colloidal state with water through pipelines in Brazil and India. If the colloidal condition breaks, solids will immediately settle down and the pipe running for more than 300 kilometres will get choked.

In a colloidal concrete process, the whole space to be concreted is first cleaned and enclosed with formwork. If required, the help of divers is taken. These divers go down deep in the water with the help of compressed air supplied for breathing and fix properly the formwork of the foundation and clean them with high-pressure air-water jets. Once the formwork is ready, it is filled with aggregates. While filling with aggregates, a few 75 to 100 mm diameter pipes are left loosely embedded in the aggregates at 3 to 4-meter spacing, keeping the bottom of the pipe at the bottom of foundation and the top above water. Grout in colloidal form is injected at a pressure of at least 3 bar plus head of water in the area to be concreted. This grout is either a neat cement grout mix of water and cement with a water/cement ratio as low as 0.35:1 or sand cement mix grout with sand/cement ratio of 3:1.

There are special colcrete grout mixer machines. They have two mixing and agitating drums. In the first mixer, water is first filled and agitated. Then, cement and sand are added while the water is still agitating. Once the water, cement and sand are uniformly mixed, the whole mix is transferred to the second drum, agitating in a much-higher speed and pumped into the aggregate base through one of the pipes. The whole process takes less than five minutes. The grout spreads in the base first and slowly comes up, replacing the water. The grout is pumped through all the pipes in rotation for uniform distribution in area to be concreted. For large foundations, multiple pumps are operated simultaneously. In this process, the grout is pushed from the bottom to the top. Hence, water does not wash the grout except for some at the top, which is ultimately washed away. Colcrete grout mixers are generally patented and available all over the world.

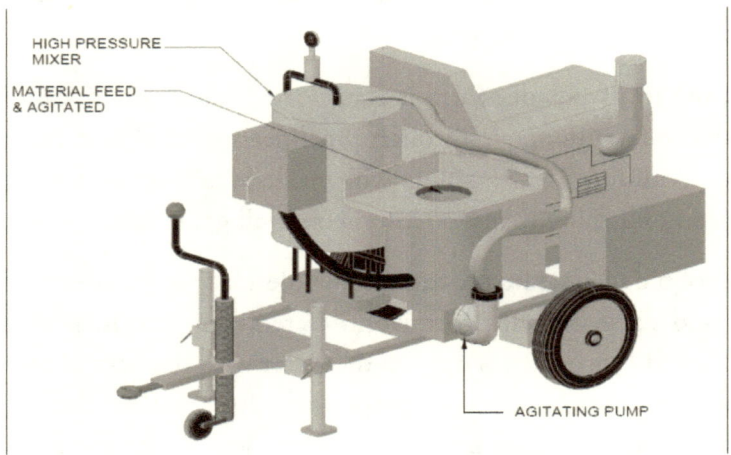

Pipes are slowly lifted as required and removed after the pumping operation is over. Within two to three days, the concrete is set.

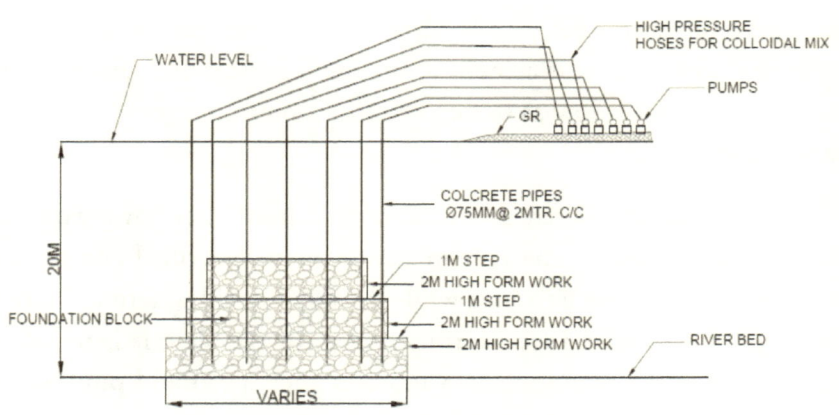

The layout of a large subsea foundation to be filled with colcrete is shown above. Multiple pumps are used due to a large foundation and each pump will feed a full row of pipes for the foundation in a designed sequence for homogeneous distribution of grout in entire foundation.

It would be preferred to plan such colcrete in stages of two meters' height, unless unavoidable, since fixing formwork, re-bars and other preparatory works are easier to manage with maximum of two meters' height underwater.

For higher foundations, a complete prefabricated form has to be lowered into the sea by a crane. This form should have enough stiffeners thoroughly welded to the steel formwork. First, while lowering the form into the water, there is heavy turbulence which shakes the form. Secondly, when filled with rock, the rock will hit the supports and is likely to break them. Thirdly, if the ground is not well-prepared and levelled, the form will sit unevenly and extra stress would be developed. These factors are to be considered in fabrication and handling the formwork.

On one of the port projects, a foundation with the pile was to be built underwater for concreting raft foundation over piles; a big steel formwork was made. The site engineer designed and fabricated the form with steel plates and timber struts jam fixed inside. While lowering the form, due to turbulence, all the struts became loose and collapsed within the form. The form was broken badly and rejected.

In the above and all other underwater concrete operations, care has to be taken to ensure that concrete does not mix with water. However, some concrete does mix with water and is rejected/made to wash away by the system/process.

7.2.6 Tremie concrete–underwater concreting for small foundations and *in situ* piles

Tremie concrete is a procedure used to carry out concreting operations underwater for small, deep foundations, columns and cast *in situ* deep piles on all locations containing a high portion of subsoil water in the piles and similar structures in the prefixed forms. One has to take care of the following while doing underwater concreting:

- Concrete should not be segregated. This is achieved by conveying the concrete through a narrow pipe and the entire mass must travel together, without any big air or water pockets, and get deposited in its confined place.

- Concrete, as finally poured, should not mix with clay and other rubbish at the bottom of the foundation and must not be washed by the water around it.

To take care of both these requirements, Tremie concrete is done for foundations as explained hereunder:

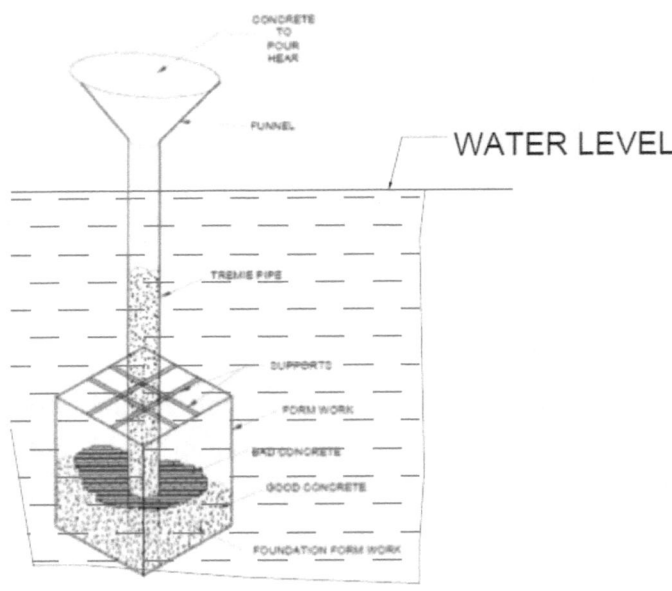

- In this system, to concrete underwater, a steel pipe is fabricated with a funnel on top as shown in the sketch. This pipe is called the Tremie pipe. The total length of the Tremie pipe is the depth of the foundation or pile, plus a few meters so as to always be above the ground or water level. For deep pile foundations, Tremie pipe is made in sections of about three meters and screwed together. The diameter of the pipe and the size of the funnel, are decided on the basis that the volume of the funnel plus the pipe, should be—if not more than—at least equal to at least half meter height of the concrete in the foundation. Further, the diameter of the pipe should not be less than 125 mm for concrete with a maximum 25 mm aggregate size.

- Once the foundation is ready for concreting, the rebar cage is first lowered into the foundation.

- The Tremie pipe is lowered, touching the bed of the foundation. Water level in the pipe will be the same as outside.

- The funnel of Tremie pipe is connected to the hook of piling rig or a crane, as the situation may require.

- A rubber ball fitting tightly in the pipe is placed in Tremie at the neck of funnel and tied with a string long enough to hold onto while the concrete is poured into the funnel.

- Release the string a bit—say, one meter—at a time. The ball will move down, holding the concrete on itself. Water will not enter the concrete in the pipe since the ball is a barrier between the concrete and the water. With the weight of the concrete on the ball, the water will be pushed down.

- Continue the operation till the ball with the concrete reaches the bottom of the pipe and the funnel is also full with concrete. Release the string holding the ball and slightly shake the pipe. Due to the weight of the concrete on the ball, it will escape and come up afloat in the water.

- As the ball is released, concrete in the pipe will also be released and will be spread in the foundation, leaving at least 30-centimetre high concrete in the pipe—the same level as outside the pipe. This concrete will sweep the floor of the foundation and push above with all the rubbish mixed with first layer of the concrete since it will be flowing in the foundation from the bottom towards the top.

- This will be followed by good concrete through the pipe as concreting proceeds.

- Concrete is passed through the Tremie pipe since the end of the pipe is buried in wet concrete. The concrete will come out of the pipe at the bottom of the foundation and move upwards pushing the earlier concrete and so the bad concrete mixed with impurities will always be on top. After some time, the concrete will not go down. Lift the pipe a little carefully, so that bottom does not come out of the wet concrete, and the concrete will slip down. This process is continued till the end. Bad concrete is either washed away or is found in the upper portion of the pile. It should be broken and discarded.

Tremie concrete is not advisable for large open subsea foundations since it would be difficult to always maintain the column of concrete in the Tremie pipe, resulting in bad concrete mixing with good concrete. Thus, colcrete is preferred for large foundations and Tremie concrete for small foundations and *in situ* pile concreting. Still, if colcrete system is unavailable, a big foundation should be divided into manageable compartments and concreted one after another by the Tremie method.

- Hand operations.

- That necessary steel re-bars are fixed for starting work.

- Wet the forms with a good spray of water and clean if there is any rubbish around.

Keep a sufficient number of crowbars for emergency on the deck, distributed between a few locations.

7.2.7 Slip form concrete for vertical structures

As its name suggests, slip form concrete is a method of concreting where the formwork of the concrete keeps on slipping upwards on the sides of the freshly-laid concrete as **concrete is poured for days together without stopping the concrete operation or changing the formwork.** In the process, enough wet concrete is maintained in the forms at all times till the required height of the structure is achieved and the concrete pouring is stopped.

If the concrete pouring is to continue after a break, get the **next concrete ready** beforehand—before stopping the current concrete operation. After stopping concrete, wet concrete is levelled in the forms and extra if any is discarded. Slip forming still continues for about 90 minutes till all the concrete is set and is released from the forms but at least 8 to 10 inches partly-set/set concrete should remain in forms before stopping slip forming. Simultaneously, all the forms are levelled accurately and cleaned with necessary repairs for proper tapers in all the walls. This should not be left for the next day and necessarily, a fresh set of people have to be organized in advance to step in immediately after stoppage of concrete. For a tapered chimney structure or cooling tower, many patented designs of formworks are available. Here, we will discuss only vertical structures since the principles of slip forming are the same for all types of structures.

Earlier, screw jacks with threaded jack-climbing rods were used for the lifting of forms. Each jack was manually lifted equally by rotating/ tightening the nut of the jack.

In slip form concrete for large structures, a number of hydraulic jacks, each having a capacity of, say, three tonnes is fixed to the special forms. The total load required to be lifted while concreting number of jacks fitted to conveniently lift the entire load on the formwork and to ensure it is well distributed in entire area.

Slip form jacks

Slip form jacks are hydraulic jacks. They climb on a 30 mm steel rod in strokes of 50 mm at fixed intervals varying between two minutes and five minutes, depending upon the speed of the concrete supply and the initial setting time of the concrete. If the concrete supply is slow, the formwork is lifted slowly and the slip-forming cycle of lifting the formwork is changed. Similarly, if the concrete is not setting fast, forms are lifted slowly. These jacks have two sets of jaws—one at the bottom and another on top. There is a vertical hole in the centre of the jack where a heavy-duty pipe measuring about 30 mm diameter—termed as slip form rods—is fitted in the jack. The jack climbs on this rod only in the upward direction, holding the rod firmly in one of its jaws. These slip form rods stand vertically on the base of the structure in four to six meters' heights and are extended as the concrete progresses by joining a new pipe with threaded studs.

When hydraulic pressure is given to the jack, the cylinder between the two jaws expands by 50 mm by putting downward pressure on the piston and bottom jaws. As the slip form rod is firmly seated on the base, it cannot go downwards. Hence, it pushes the jacks upwards. Top jaw of jack climbs 50 mm on slip form rods along with entire setup fitted on the platform and then hold the rod firmly. At a preset pressure, the hydraulic pump trips automatically. On release of pressure, the bottom jaw would move up by 50 mm to its original position. By then, the upper jaw would hold the climbing rod and not allow any slipping. Pump will restart as per the timer and again, the jack will climb by 50 mm. The jack keeps on climbing on the rod, step-by-step. This exercise continues till concreting is finished. This process is similar to a man climbing on a coconut or palm tree, embracing the tree firmly with his hands and feet. Lifting of form less than 50 mm at one time is not desirable since, for every lift, the formwork has to break any bond it has with the wet concrete. Hence, a minimum lift of 50 mm at one time is desirable. However, in some brands of jacks, this can be adjustable for different lift strokes.

Form Work

Concrete takes about forty-five minutes to set or become solid from the time of pouring into the formwork. Forms are one-meter high and 750 mm concrete is always in the formwork while concreting is in progress and is continuously poured in the form. Considering a 50 mm lift every three minutes to be the highest speed for moving concrete out of the formwork from the time of pouring, it will need fifteen strokes every three minutes; that makes forty-five minutes. It means that the concrete is set in the formwork before it comes out of it. For a speed slower than three minutes, the concrete speed has to be slow and all the forms should always be filled at the same level.

Reinforcement steel bars are also tied simultaneously as concrete progresses and the forms move upward. These bars provide additional support to the concrete. The speed of lifting the forms is adjusted according to atmospheric temperature and supply of concrete, as stated above.

Concrete, once out of the form, should not bulge as well as should not be solid and stick to the form. The form must keep on moving without stopping and slipping on the concrete. If the speed of lifting is slow and the concrete sticks to the form, it means that the friction created between the concrete and the form is much higher than the tear strength of the concrete at that time;, the jack will still lift the form and tear off the concrete, carrying set concrete with it. If not repaired immediately by releasing concrete from the form by breaking with crowbars, the jack will continue to lift the set concrete with increase in quantity every time, thus increasing the load on the jack. Ultimately, the jack will stop working due to excessive load created by the increase of friction between the form and the concrete. This will spread like cancer since the surrounding jacks have to take additional load due to failure of that jack. Within a few minutes, more jacks will stop lifting and the form level will become highly distorted. Ultimately, the slip forming operation will collapse soon. In cold climates, the speed of the formwork is to be reduced for allowing initial set of concrete within the form or some additives are to be added in the concrete.

A few important issues for slip form concrete

- Consistent supply of quality concrete for long duration in a single operation.

- Adequate supply of raw materials to be available at batching plant on a non-stop basis from stocks. Hence, a full quantity of all the material must be in stock before the start of the concrete and must remain available till finish.

- Re-bars cut to size must be available at site with arrangement for continuous fixing as concrete proceeds.

- Change of shifts and relievers on the job for entire workforce including management to be in roster. There was a failure in 1974 on Goa port project due to an overworked expert going to sleep for two hours.

- Distribution of concrete uniformly in all the forms must be ensured.

- Power backup and repairs management to be done.

- It is to be ensured that all the jacks are going up with a uniform level of forms. In case of any distortions, it should be rectified at the earliest possible.

- Continuous trowel finish and touch-ups to be done to the outside surface to set the concrete.

- In case of problems, a planned shutdown is to be taken under expert directions and supervision.

If done properly, a 17-metre high seaport foundation having 28 vertical compartments with almost 220 jacks working together can be finished in less than two days with the consistent supply of concrete on an average of 20 cubic meters per hour and re-bars 12 tonnes per hour in floating condition including the time spent for start-up and closing down activities. Way back in 1972 in Visakhapatnam Port, this technology was first used for the construction of an ore berth and then this technology was continually used in India on many port projects for many years, successfully. The photographs illustrated below are from the Marmugao port project in 1974/75. For taller concrete structures, planned breaks are necessary due to limitations of structural strength in fresh concrete and management constraints.

Formwork assembly for slip forming

We have shown the typical formwork used for a structure having walls of 250 mm thickness. Formwork is preferably made with close-grained, seasoned timber of 40 mm × 125 to 150 mm × 1 metre long planks, free of knots. These planks are joined together by tongue and groove joints nailed on two hard wood, seasoned and straight runners measuring 150 mm × 100 mm in section. In case of a curvature in the structure, like the circular sections or corners of a caisson, two numbers of 200 mm × 50 mm are used. Timber planks are cut to the desired profile and nailed together with staggered joints. All timber planks of 40 mm thickness must be nailed in the form keeping timber vanes going downwards to avoid extra friction by timber on fresh concrete and its fast wearing out. If one moves his hand on the plank upside down, it would be along the vanes and would provide a smooth feeling but if he moves it in the opposite direction, the ends of the vanes would create friction and hurt. All planks and 150 × 100 timber runners should be planed straight on both sides with uniform thickness maintained. Keep a clear distance of 200 mm from the top of the form to the upper runner and the same from the bottom of the form to the lower runner.

Take the forms on the raft foundation and assemble on a level surface in position with temporary supports. If the wall's thickness is 250 mm, the spacing between the forms in the bottom would be 252 and 247 mm on top. Forms are fixed in their conical shape to reduce friction while the concrete is moving in the form.

Fix the yoke and channels as per the design of the slip form equipment supplier and nail them properly to the lower runner of the forms. The jack will be loosely but firmly placed under the bottom of the channel of yoke assembly. While working, the jack will push the channels upward. In turn, the channel will push the yoke assembly to move upward along with forms and the entire infrastructure will lift, leaving the concrete in place. On top of formwork, there usually is a deck for working and other fittings it is generally made as per the following drawing, with small changes as per the requirements of the suppliers of the equipment. A covered deck, in addition to the work platform, arrests the heat generated by the fresh concrete below the formwork and helps in fast gaining of strength after initial set. Reinforcement bars guide and mason the hanging platforms fixed for ease of operations and for the finishing of surface to be carried out simultaneously.

Timber forms are preferred to steel forms due to the following reasons:

- Steel forms become very hot and difficult to work with after some time

- Linear expansion of steel due to heat is more compared to timber

- Timber forms are easier to repair while concreting is in progress

- Steel forms, unless made of thick plates, which are heavy, get kinks in handling it is not acceptable for slip forming since fresh concrete would get into the kinks and create extra friction.

If handled carefully, steel forms could have multiple uses, while timber forms are good only for one use. Second use is partly possible if handled very carefully and not damaged while slip forming.

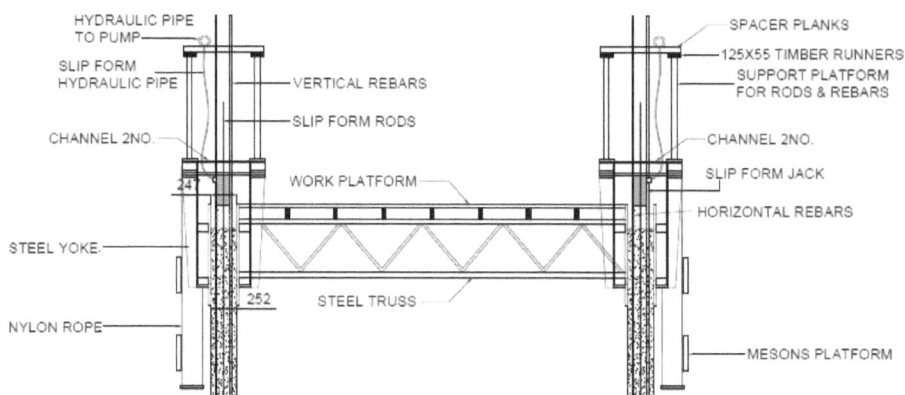

Troubleshooting and precautions in slip form concrete

Including friction loads and men working on top is equally distributed between the sufficient nu

Before we start out with pouring concrete, the following things are to be checked:

- That all materials required for the pour are available on site with extra backup.

- That all equipment is properly serviced with fuel and lubricants available in sufficient quantities for the operation.

- That all labour and supervision staff is properly planned in shifts with definite logistic arrangements.

- Proper lights for the night are organized. Do a trial the previous night.

- That concrete equipment like buckets are serviced and in good shape.

- The level of the form by levelling the instrument or water tubes.

- The taper of each form at least at two meters' distance and correct if there is any discrepancy.

- The hydraulic tank of the slip form system with all the pipes are full with oil and beaded it for any air pockets. For air bleeding, the pump is started at a very low pressure without disturbing the forms and the hydraulic oil inlet of each jack is opened and beaded.

- All the slip form rods are standing firmly on the base and the jacks are touching the channels of yoke assembly. Rods to go down with a small push by

Now, start the concrete in 150 mm layers spread uniformly in the entire form. The first lift of 50 mm to the form is given after 20 minutes or a maximum of 30 minutes of starting concrete and at least 30 cm of concrete should be available evenly in all the forms. Attend to any discrepancy, proceed and continue as stated above till the finish of work. There may be some reverse slopes. In such cases, the concrete will crack. Repair the formwork immediately.

In this image, concreting of a float precast concrete foundation (Caisson) is in progress in Goa, a port in India, in 1974. Concrete is poured from a bucket fixed to a floating crane on the right side. On the left is a barge carrying steel bars. Vertical lines are for re-bars and slip form jack rods. The horizontal line on top consists of supports for re-bars and rods, keeping them straight. The two horizontal lines show the slip form. The bottom line is for masons to inspect. A hut on the right of the concrete bucket is the hydraulic pumping station to which power is fed by generators on a crane barge.

7.2.8 Slip form concrete in road pavements/canal concrete lining

Roads and highways are classified into two categories—rigid pavements like concrete roads and flexible pavements such as asphalt roads and others like Water Bond Macadam roads. Concrete roads are also called rigid pavements. They are durable if the sub-structure up to the base course does not settle or sink for any reason including landslides, poor construction, inadequate drainage, etc. In case of settlements due to these problems, a big part of the road's concrete is cracked and settled and hence discarded, removed and redone. It needs to be redone after the removal of the affected concrete with heavy equipment. In case of flexible pavements, the top of the road adjusts with the settlements and the road is still usable, but it will not be comfortable due to its uneven surface. Repairs are cheap. It just needs the filling up of depressions with asphalt concrete or approved material. For new roads, unless very good quality control measures are adopted, it is advisable to make flexible pavements and after a few years of good usage and settlements, if any, to convert them into rigid pavements.

For concrete roads, the following things must be done:

- The road foundation up to the base course is prepared. This is common for flexible and rigid pavements.

- Concrete pavements are made *in situ* concrete slabs of a required thickness, touching each other with the provision of expansion joints as designed.

- The top surface of these concrete slabs is finished manually and, despite all the care, some level differences are unavoidable.

- These uneven levels in the road surface are not comfortable for driving and are noticeable at high speeds due to jerks on uneven surfaces.

- A few engineers provide a 50 mm topping of asphalt for better driving comfort. This takes care of uneven concrete surfaces and wearing off of weak road surface due to segregation in concrete while pouring, bad curing and inadequate cement content.

- Due to direct dumping by transit mixers on ground, big stones get separated from the concrete and are thrown a little away. Only slurry drops remain in a heap on the ground. The masons drag these stones in the concrete but the mix is not homogeneous. This is called segregation of concrete. They should remix with a spade mortar and loose aggregates mix thoroughly and then do the placements.

- Segregation of concrete reduces the quality and some weak pockets are formed.

- These weak pockets create potholes on the road after some time. It puts a question mark on the capabilities of the contractor, due to the negligence of the mason and the supervising engineer. It takes only a few minutes to mix the wet concrete by a few people with spades.

Slip form road pavements

- Now, slip form concrete pavers are available. Concrete is poured in the hopper of the paver machine from the back and the paver spreads concrete evenly in the front while moving back for the full width of the road.

- The level of concrete surface is monitored by a fine metallic wire attached to a slip form paver, which maintains a uniform level of concrete as per the profile of the road. A sensor travels on a wire as the paver is moved and adjusts the concrete paving height, keeping the top of the concrete on level with the wire. The better the more undisturbed the wire profiles in firm supports, the better the concrete surface.

- The concrete is free of segregations since it is mixed again in the paver machine.

- Here, the supply rate of concrete has to be large and should be maintained throughout the paving operation.

- This system gives the road a machine finish. It is smooth, levelled and durable. The entire section of the road concreting can be done in one operation and up to half a kilometre of road can be completed in one shift.

- Slip form speed is to be maintained at a minimum of 30 to 40 meters per hour for the whole two-lane carriageway. In case of constrains in concrete supply, half the road width is taken at a time.

- Concrete roads last longer than 80 years without maintenance if done properly. Though they are 25 to 50% more expensive, it is overall a cheaper and preferred if the investment is available

- Similarly, the base and sides of big canals are concreted by the same slip form pavers.

From one side of the paver, concrete is poured on the base course using transit mixers and the other picture shows finished concrete by the slip form paver.

For slopes of canals, paver is fixed tilted in alignment with the canal.

08

Opencast and Underwater Rock Blasting

Hard rock, which is difficult to break using crowbars or other mechanical means—including normal excavators—is broken into small pieces by blasting.

Blasting operations are carried out by the use of explosives. It needs qualified personnel to carry, store and use these explosives safely, with utmost care. These experts are trained at job sites by qualified instructors and licenses are given after the department of explosives conducts exams. Unauthorized possession or use of explosives warrants severe punishment including jail for a few years.

Blasting and haulage operations are classified into three types, depending upon the situations.

- Blasting in open-to-sky areas, hills and open pits are called opencast mining.

- Blasting in tunnels and underground structures is called underground mining.

- Blasting in river beds and subsea conditions with a big cover of water is called underwater rock blasting.

The principles of blasting operations are the same for all the locations but are a risk to life and surroundings but the equipment and methods used in different locations are different, depending upon the situation.

First, a hole of minimum 28 mm diameter is drilled at the location of the blast by a drill machine preferably operated by compressed air. Compressed air is used to provide rotation and hammering to the drilling tool and also to flush clean the drill hole. This is done by passing compressed air in a hole in the drilling tool while drilling is in progress.

Compressed air is preferred to electricity to avoid short circuits or sparks due to any reasons in the areas near the explosives—which may cause explosion.

For construction sites, safer explosives classified as class-three explosives are used which do not explode if carefully handled and generation of sparks while hitting is avoided. Hence steel rods, shoes with nails or leather sole and other such objects which may create a spark by rubbing/hitting are not permitted while handling explosives. Cigarettes and matchboxes are totally prohibited.

Explosives used in construction are done so in two parts; one is gelatine or any other similar explosive and a detonator. In each hole, sufficient quantity of gelatine is filled up, well-compacted by the wooden tamping sticks put into the hole, measuring up to about two-thirds the depth of hole and one detonator is placed at bottom of the hole. This detonator has a long electric wire and detonates by a spark created inside the detonator by passing a 12-volt current through this wire. With the detonation of the detonator, the entire explosive will instantaneously become gas, creating huge pressure, and break the rock into pieces while gas is released in atmosphere. These rock pieces also fly off far and wide. Therefore, due care has to be taken while blasting and the area is cleared up to a safe distance all around the blast location before blast. The blasting crew takes cover at a safe location. The area is cleared for entry of others after checking whether the blast is entirely completed and if all the explosives used are entirely burned.

Each hole will have a separate detonator. All the detonator wires are connected to each other and are blasted together in a single, large location.

Detonators are never carried or stored together with the explosives, batteries, tools and other dangerous objects and can blast with heavy damages if hit by a small hammer. They are always carried in separate vehicles and stored away from the explosives in different stores. Even the storage place, called a magazine, has to be built as per the rules of the department of explosives and they too have their own requisites like approval and license to store. These magazines are built as per the specifications provided by the department of explosives in remote places with nobody living within 2 to 5 kilometres all around, depending on the size of the magazine and the types of explosives being stored. The whole magazine may blast due to hitting of lightening or mishandling.

Opencast quarrying/mining

For open cast mining, a few benches are created on the hill face. The height of each face should not be more than the point where the excavator bucket is able to reach. This is important for the safety of the entire operation and equipment. Sometimes, after blasting, big boulders remain stuck on top of the bench and need careful handling by the operator. Hence, all possible boulder hangouts should be within the safe reach of the excavator

Underwater blasting

For underwater blasting operations, a jack-up platform is used to drill holes in the sea bed and charging explosives. Multiple holes are drilled at one location and after drilling and loading the explosives is completed, this platform is shifted to a safe location before blasting.

Such platforms are floating barges that operate on four legs and can be lifted above water by lowering these legs by hydraulic jacks/winches. Blasted material is dredged (removed) by a crane with grabs (buckets which dig into blasted material) mounted on simple, floating barges.

We have intentionally not deliberated here the various methods of use and the types of explosives, for safety reasons.

09

Structural Steel Fabrication

Steel bridges, warehouses, tall buildings and industrial structures are built by joining different steel sections like angles, girders, rods, plates and others as per the design, alignments, shapes and sizes prepared by the engineers. These structures are called steel structures and the **process** of building these structures from raw material like angles, girders, etc., is called **structural steel fabrication.**

Steel sections like rods, angles, girders, plates, etc. are available in different grades and strengths. The strength of a steel section depends on selection of proportions of different raw material like Iron, carbon, nickel, cobalt, etc., while manufacturing it. Accordingly, a grade is assigned to this steel. This steel of a particular grade will have defined qualities of strength in different applications. Tensile strength is the strength at which this item will lose strength and become like plastic. On pulling, sheer strength is the force that is required to break it in two pieces. Manufacturers provide a test certificate with every consignment for actual properties of steel supplied and for important structures, it is desired to get a few samples get tested in a laboratory for own satisfaction in presence of buyer's representative. All major and medium-size mills have such testing facility. Just cut a few pieces from the product and get them tested for elongation, bending and shear.

9.1 Fabrication

First, a list of sizes, grades and quantities of all the steel sections required is prepared from drawings and ordered by the workshop.

A workshop is a covered shed with enough open space in front and the sides for fabrication and storage of raw material and finished products.

It is also attached to a small, covered paint shop. The paint shop is covered to avoid dust sticking to fresh paint and to avoid paint mixing with air and spreading far and wide, polluting the atmosphere. All the workers for in the paint shop should have eye protection goggles and breathing masks.

The weld shop should also have protective gear as specified for workers.

A workshop, generally, has the following equipment.

An overhead travelling crane is used to lift and shift fabricated items from one place to the other. For bigger workshops, it can be a fully electrically-operated travelling crane but for small jobs, one can also manage with hand-operated chain pulley blocks, even up to ten tonnes capacity travelling on a girder.

A pillar drilling machine for drilling holes in steel sections plus a few hand-held small drill machines are present.

Cutting tools could be small shearing machines, cutting steel blades, handheld or power-operated and a gas cutting set preferably with a pug cutting machine.

Gas cutting set has a torch. Oxygen and acetylene gas is fed to this torch and a flame is made at the nozzle of the torch while maintaining a balance of oxygen and acetylene. A technician will heat the steel section at the point of cutting. On sufficient heating, he will inject more oxygen onto the heated section. This oxygen will convert a small portion of steel into slag and slag will flow down, cutting the steel pieces into two pieces.

A small training course is necessary to operate this cutting torch. Oxygen and acetylene are available in the market filled in cylinders. Cooking gas can also be used instead of acetylene gas.

9.1.1 Joining steel sections

Steel sections in different shapes and sizes are joined together to fabricate a steel structure. These sections are bolted, riveted or welded at the joints.

9.1.2 Bolting and riveting

Bolting is done simply by drilling holes on both pieces, inserting a bolt with nut through it and tightening it. The joint can be opened at any time by removing the bolts. It further loosens due to vibrations after some time. To avoid loosening, additional nuts and/or split pins are used.

If these joints are of a permanent nature and not required to be opened at any time, riveting instead of bolting is preferred. Bolts could become loose with time due to many reasons and easier to sabotage. Riveting is a little cumbersome; it requires shanks, bolt-like steel pieces which have a head on one side, are red-heated, inserted in the holes and hammered flat to the shape of a bolt head on the other side, with a tight grip on the joint.

9.1.3 Welding

For making a permanent joint in two pieces of any metal, welding is the most common procedure adopted. Both the metal pieces are cleaned near the joint and are to be free of dirt, rust or any other material. They are placed together in shape and size as per the drawing and welded with a welding machine as per specifications and directions. A welding machine is an electrical generator or transformer producing direct current **at a low voltage but high amperes. The** negative terminal of output of a welding machine is connected to one of the steel pieces to be welded. The positive terminal is connected to a welding holder with a long cable. This special, single-core, insulated cable is good for high currents at a low voltage. A qualified and experienced welder will take a welding rod, hold one side with the holder and the other side will point the joint to be welded. A big spark will be created and maintained by the welder by carefully handling the welding electrode. The joint will be heated by this spark and the metal of the electrode will melt and get deposited on the joint, making metals of both the sections completely monolithic with the addition of metal deposited by electrode; this is how a joint is created. Thickness of metal deposited in the joint by burning the electrode should be more than the thickness of the thinnest section to be welded. Joints are ground in particular shapes as per the design. Generally, it is in a "V" shape with about a2 mm gap at the bottom.

These electrodes have a thick coating of a powder-like substance. This helps maintain the flame and creates a gas chamber around the electrode tip to avoid oxygen in the air mixing with the metal. If air comes in contact with molten steel or any other metal, it will turn the metal into oxide and some metal will be wasted.

This spark/flame is very bright and harmful to the eyes. Therefore, a welder uses a shield and on-lookers should not look at the flame. Further, the coatings on these electrodes produce some fumes that are not good for health.

Electrodes have same metal as of the items to be joined, hence available in different quality and grades. For thick sections, thick electrode and high current is required, while for thinner sections, thin electrodes and low currents are necessary.

For very thin metals and metallic ornaments etc., small flames created by any of the many common methods like a flame created by candle and joint is heated and welded by help of an electrode of the same metal.

Joining of plastic sheets and other material by heating process is also called welding.

9.2 Painting

Steel and some other metals get rusted if left in the open for a long time and get deteriorated. Iron in the open draws oxygen from the atmosphere and makes iron oxide, known as rust. This rust drops off with small tempering or rubbing with a wire brush and slowly, the steel item becomes thinner and thinner, losing strength.

To avoid rusting, steel is painted after fabrication is completed. Paints are generally oils mixed with chemicals as per the requirements of different applications depending upon the metal to be painted and the environment around the where the painted structure is to live in. Selection of paint and its application procedure is done by a knowledgeable person or as per the directions of the paint manufacturer. They provide necessary documents with each supply of paint.

Before painting, the steel structure's surface is cleaned properly with a wire brush. Other methods like sandblasting, shot blasting or special chemical applications are also used.

Sandblasting is done by mechanically hitting the surface very hard with a mix of compressed air and thick sand. In turn, all the rust, etc., is removed from the surface by continuous hitting the sand particles with a high force. It is thoroughly cleaned for loose particles before painting.

In shot blasting, metallic granules are used instead of sand. If sand has wet clay particles, they stick to the steel surface in thin layers; this is not desirable.

Painting is done with generally three coats of paints; the first coat is called a primer and prepares the base for the paint.

If painting is done on an unclean surface, this undesirable dirt and material on the steel will act as a barrier between the steel surface and paint, and the paint will peel off after some time.

In your own house, if oil paint is applied on a wet wall, the paint will peel off after the water dries off.

9.3 Transport of fabricated steel structures

Once fabrication and painting are completed, the structure is shifted to the location of its placement by trailers and trucks. Care is to be taken for following:

The structure should not disfigure in handling and transport.

The structure should be covered by thick jute/plastic or cloth at points of contact with transport vehicle and ropes used for tying and lifting to avoid paint damages.

Size and weight of the structure to be transported should be manageable. If necessary, one could divide the structures into smaller pieces for safe transportation.

9.4 Erection of steel and other structures

Lifting, shifting and fixing at the desired location at different heights have always been a challenge for engineers of all ages.

In the prehistoric period, and even for centuries thereafter, fixing any article at certain heights required an earthen ramp to be built on one side of the monument and items to be fixed were made in small pieces and shifted to the location on mules and donkeys through this ramp for erection and joining.

The ramp used to be raised in stages by putting more earth as the structure was built higher. After completion of the project, the ramp was dismantled and the earth from it was disposed in a nearby area.

9.4.1 Levers

It is impossible to say who **invented** the first mechanical **lever**. Humans have used mechanical **levers** since the Stone Age. The earliest remaining writings regarding **levers** date back to the 3rd century BC and were provided by Archimedes.

Some people say that Archimedes once said something like "Give me a stick and a place to stand, and I shall move the world." If he really did say this, it was with good reason. Thanks to Archimedes, we understood the law of the lever.

These force multipliers are called simple machines. A simple machine is a basic mechanical device that changes the magnitude or direction of a force to a very big extent.

A hand cart is an ideal case of using the theory of lever in daily use. One puts heavier items near the wheel or fulcrum and smaller items a bit away as shown in the sketch. If you load heavier items near the handle, you may not even be able to lift the cart.

Hand cart   **Archimedes imagination to lift the Earth by using a long lever**

Distance of load from the wheel axel (pivot) multiplied by load on cart is equal to distance of handle multiplied by the load applied on handle.

However, a discount has to be given for load kept on handle side of cart as shown in the above drawing.

If distance of hand is six times more than distance of load from pivot on other side of pivot, one could lift six times heavier load than efforts to lift directly without the use of a cart.

9.4.2 Chain pulley blocks

Small lifts up to two or three meters, weighing up to 15 to 20 tonnes are made by simple chain pulley blocks. The chain pulley block is hung firmly to a tripod or 'A' frame and the item is lifted by hooking it to the other end of the chain pulley block by two or three persons working together. By pulling the smaller chain in one direction, the load is lifted and by pulling it in reverse, the load is lowered down.

Chain pulley block of 15 tonnes capacity

9.4.3 Winches and pulleys

Bigger weights which cannot be done by a chain pulley block are lifted or moved by winches which could be hand-operated or diesel-power driven. In addition, a set of pulleys are introduced in the system for lifting loads many times higher than the capacity of the winch.

A typical hand winch

Load is applied through a rope tied to a big drum. The drum rotates as load is applied by hand on the handle. Pulling force on the rope applied through the winch would be equal to the load applied by hand and multiplied by gear ratio of the two gears shown in the photo.

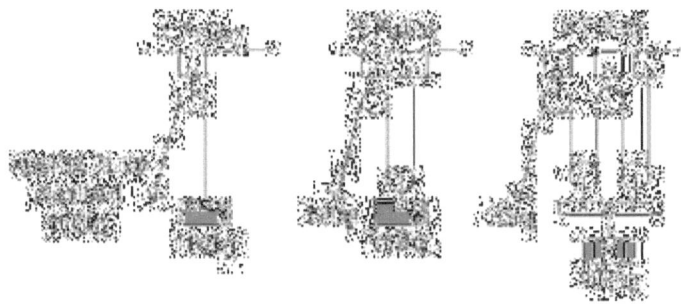

In addition to the multiplier effect of the winch, if some pulley is introduced between the winch and the load to be handled, the load-carrying capacity of the combined system will increase in multiplications as shown in the above pulley configurations. For illustration, 100 kgs, 50 kgs and 25 kgs are forces applied on the winch.

These winches are freely available in the market, up to ten tonnes in capacity. They are hand-operated and for higher capacities, diesel or electric-driven motors are required.

9.4.4 Jim poles

For erection of structures in open spaces, long, heavy-duty steel posts are erected near the location of erection. These poles are tied with four ropes anchored in the ground on all the four sides of the post and the pulley system is fixed on top of these posts for erection purposes. In complicated erections, even two or more poles are used connected together in a predesigned configuration.

These are a few tools and there are many innovative methods for the erection of heavy structures without proper means and resources. Each one of these methods is tailor-made for any situation.

9.4.5 Erection by crane

Erection by a crane of adequate capacity is the easiest method of erection, provided such a crane is available.

For erection of heavy structures, many operators are generally available and without adequate knowledge and experience, one should not do such risky works.

All cranes have a standard lifting capacity. This is the load the crane can lift with the standard length of boom at a particular radius. This capacity reduces with increase in length of the boom and increase in the radius.

The typical load chart of a crane is illustrated below. In this chart, the load lifting capacity is given for different lengths of boom with different radius of the same crane.

OPERATING RADIUS (FT)	BOOM LENGTH											
	27 FT		34 FT		43 FT		52 FT		61 FT		70 FT	
	LOADED BOOM ANGLE (DEG)	LOAD RATING (LB)	LOADED BOOM ANGLE (DEG)	LOAD RATING (LB)	LOADED BOOM ANGLE (DEG)	LOAD RATING (LB)	LOADED BOOM ANGLE (DEG)	LOAD RATING (LB)	LOADED BOOM ANGLE (DEG)	LOAD RATING (LB)	LOADED BOOM ANGLE (DEG)	LOAD RATING (LB)
5	77	34,000										
10	66	21,100	71	17,100	75	16,000	78	15,700				
15	54	15,100	62	14,000	68	12,100	72	11,100	75	10,800	77	9,600
20	39	11,100	51	10,100	61	9,100	66	8,600	71	8,200	73	7,300
25	17	7,900	40	7,700	53	7,100	61	6,900	66	6,600	69	5,900
30			23	6,500	44	6,100	54	5,600	60	5,300	64	4,900
35					33	4,800	47	4,700	54	4,600	60	4,150
40					16	3,500	38	4,100	48	3,900	55	3,550
45							27	3,250	41	3,200	49	3,050
50	NOTE: RATINGS ABOVE THE HEAVY LINE ARE BASED ON STRUCTURAL COMPETENCE AND NOT ON MACHINE STABILITY.						9	2,950	33	2,800	44	2,650
55									23	2,500	37	2,350
60											29	1,900
65											19	1,700

Stowed Jib Deductions (Pounds)

450	360	260	230	200	175

One can notice that the capacity of this crane with 27-foot boom and a five-foot operating radius is 34000 pounds, while it reduces to 1700 pounds when operating with 70-foot boom at a 65-foot radius. This crane will be classified as a crane with a 34000-pound capacity.

Crane has to be positioned at a safe spot for lifting and erection of a particular piece of structure at a distance and height and accordingly, a suitable crane is chosen to lift heaviest piece of structure. Further crane gives better results if tracks are parallel to boom. Distance is measured from the centre of the crane body.

Crane capacity changes with direction of pads and boom. Hence, when the operator lifts a structure for erection, he will first reduce the operating radius by bringing the load nearer to the crane. Then, he will slowly swing to the direction of erection and then adjust the radius and lift the structure for erection and position it in the desired location of erection.

10

Construction Method Statement for the Project

For a project, once the scope of work, specifications and time frame for completion of the project is confirmed, the contractor has to first generate a construction method statement for the project for his own satisfaction; detailed planning and costing is interrelated to this method statement.

Once the method statement is prepared, a plan is drawn on how and in how much time the project will be executed.

On the basis of this planning, the quantities of work to be done for all the activities is tabulated for each activity of the project and the resources required to carry out all the activities are calculated and compiled in an easily-understandable statement by the planning engineer.

Once time and resources, including men, material and equipment are available, the cost can be easily worked out.

Often clients also ask for this well-documented statement for their perusal. After detailed discussions and approval of the method statement, resources deployment and final price for the project is given to the client incorporating the outcome of all discussions.

Decision of consideration for the award of a contract is subject to fulfilment of conditions including past experience, resource mobilization plans, time schedule and the method statement. Price is taken in a separate sealed cover and is opened after satisfactorily approval of all other conditions.

If major changes in time schedule, etc., are to be made by the contractor, the client should allow the contractor to revise the price, if considered necessary, before opening bid prices of all the contractors.

Hence, once indicated that the contractor is in run and is likely to be considered for the award of the contract, the contractor, his project manager or planner studies the document carefully.

He also:

- Makes a site visit if not done earlier.

- Takes an account of all the resources and expertise available in-house.

- He and his team, with their experience and innovative skills, work out a system or method as to how they would execute the project.

- Draw out a rough time schedule for the project.

- Resources required for completing it as per time schedule.

- Cost of project, i.e., funds required to complete as per this system, resources and time schedule.

- Open discussions within company's management team including the project manager.

- Incorporations of suggestions and revisit the viability and merits of its final outcome. It is the Project Manager's final decision to accept any or all the changes recommended but however, he should give reasoning for difficulties or for not liking any particular change.

- Finally, a method statement is approved by the Project Manager with the consent of the management committee. All further planning, resource mobilization and execution planning is carried out based on this method statement.

- This method statement is submitted to the client for their approval.

- During the execution stage, the project manager makes necessary changes based on physical conditions/problems faced at the site with the knowledge of the head office and client.

- Some clients ask for the method statement with the tender but if post-tender discussions are made, then the client is under the obligation to allow a change of the method statement based on discussions.

11

Project Management

Now, we will move onto discussing practical issues with their applications for the management of a project.

11.1 Health, Safety and Environment (HSE)

With all-round development in the world, including developing countries, compliance of **HSE** requirements has become an important issue in project management. Whatever may be efficient to the contractor, he is required to maintain records of HSE compliances and this carries a good consideration in decision-making on award of future contracts to the contractor.

Good HSE compliances reduce labour unrest, better productivity, low accident rates, reduce project costs by getting more effective man-hours, less insurance premiums and reduction of medical expenses.

Environment protection is now a global issue and all over the world, more and more stringent rules are coming into force and being implemented. To date, it is very difficult to just cut a tree in one's own compound, drive a vehicle emitting black smoke or drive a truck full of mud without covering it with tarpaulin.

Health

It is the responsibility of the contractor to take care of the health of his workforce, especially as they are working in an environment deterrent to health. At first, he should provide suitable means to eliminate or reduce impact of such deterrents and then, in addition, provide medicines for protection from illnesses. In olden days, employers used to give jaggery to eat after a days' work to workers working in dusty atmosphere so as to avoid the dust inhaled that day from going to their lungs and so that it goes to their stomach while eating jaggery. Doctors wear hand gloves and cover their mouth and nose with a mask while treating infected patients. In towns having high levels of smoke pollution, traffic police now wear a face mask.

The following precautionary measures are to be taken related to general health care of employees as applicable:

- Provide adequate clean toilet facilities for workmen

- Arrange proper drainage in case of frequent rains to avoid mosquitoes and other insects from brewing at the site

- Safe, treated water for drinking and cooking

- Hygienic food preparation and serving to workforce

- Safety eyewear to be provided according to working environments

- Face masks to be used while working in dusty atmosphere

- Clean beds with good air circulation for sleeping

- Periodical medical check-ups for everybody working on the project

- Any other precaution advised by the doctor

On an airport construction project in a dense rain forest, deadly mosquitoes and frequent malaria was a matter of routine and of big concern. The client was worried of getting a proper contractor, who would take risks on his workforce. The workforce required was above 2000. The client gave the contract to Specialist Company to cordon off the site and camp areas from mosquitoes by spraying mosquito repellent chemicals regularly before mobilization of the workforce and continued thereafter till the project completion. He also made it mandatory for everybody to take an anti-malaria pill daily. In three years' working, there was zero-man hour time loss due to malaria. The total cost was less than the treatment cost of malaria for 1% i.e., twenty worker's treatment a year. All the contractors and their workmen were saved from this hazardous environment and finished the project satisfactorily on time, without any fear.

Such situations are often faced in some way or the other on green field projects at the beginning and should not be taken lightly. Else, it would create big administrative, personal health and safety problems.

Safety

Safety precautions and requirements on the project site, camp and surrounding society would be explained to the entire workforce. They will be providing a safety kit and a safety manual for the project. On a normal project site, the safety officer should insist on the following as a bare minimum:

- Use of safety shoes and helmets all the time at the workplace.

- Proper dress that is safe for work. Generally, a uniform is provided.

- Safety gloves of an adequate standard and suitable quality while doing physical work, including climbing ladders. Separate gloves are available for different applications.

- The usage of safety goggles or suitable eyewear if working in a dusty environment, or in the bright sun/light.

- Stay away from welding and gas cutting unless you are wearing protective gear and special eyewear.

- Wear safety belts as mandatory and always use them while working at heights and risky situations, ensuring they are always clamped and fixed on, stable and firm.

- Check if scaffoldings and scantlings are on stable, flat level base and erected with all joints tightened and fixed as per design and drawing. You should avoid overloading temporary as well as permanent structures. In normal circumstances, loading to design load needs elaborate checks to avoid accidents. 80 to 85% of design working load is safe depending on quality of structure to be loaded.

- Barricade the working area of cranes, excavators and similar equipment and prohibit unauthorized workmen and officers entering the barricaded area while equipment is in operation. Generally, officers get hurt more often due to overconfidence.

- Check the safe capacity and condition of lifting tackles and the crane before lifting a heavy item to ensure it is of safe capacity and not worn out or damaged.

- All cranes have a safe working capacity according to condition of the crane. Further, the capacity reduces with increase in working radius of the crane and height of the object to be lifted. The more the height, the more would be the length of the crane boom and the lesser the load lifting capacity. Lifting capacity reduces with increase in the length of the crane boom and working radius. On greater heights, wind speed and pressure are also often a big consideration.

- The crane has to stand on a stable, firm and level ground, having enough bearing capacity to take care of the loads of crane and the items to be lifted. A layer of hardwood sleepers—say, 250 mm × 300 mm × 2 metres long—under crane pads would distribute the load to bigger area and stabilize the crane. Further, the crane should never stand on muddy soil and operate. In case of mud, remove the mud, fill up with gravel, compact it and then position the crane on this platform and avoid further inflow of water by providing a drain.

- Check that the crane is safe to lift in all the positions of the crane. Capacities of cranes differ with different positions of load and more precaution has to be taken when the crane has to swing with load slowly.

- Frequently, if load is lifted in front of pads and is swung with high speed, it topples with load since it was not safe for loading on sides of pads. While swinging at high speeds, load moves a bit outward, thus increasing working radius.

- Keep the site clean as far as possible and provide good approaches.

- Keep project site adequately barricaded to avoid onlookers entering the site and getting hurt in a state of anxiety and ignorance.

- On a building project, initially, there were more than 200 spectators on daily basis, standing outside the compound for hours since this project was something new. The contractor erected a strong, see-through fencing all around so that one could see the happenings on the other side of the fence. He also posted a few security guards to spread safety awareness and thence, no problem arose.

There are many more precautions to be taken depending on the type of work and its specific requirements.

The safety officer of the contractor is responsible and monitors safety compliance and advises on the safety precautions to be taken. It is always preferred to have a knowledgeable safety officer at site. The safety officer, along with his team, gets involved while doing any work having potential risk of accidents to the structure or workers. They first give a safety briefing on safe working methods and then ensure that the work is being carried out according to these safe practices and instructions. His instructions to stop work cannot be overruled even by the Project Manager and if the Project Manager tries, the safety officer will mark a copy of his instructions to state labour department and get absolved of his responsibilities.

If the floor slab of a high-rise building is to be fixed, he would first check that all the workers are physically fit to work at that height, since many get nervous on looking down even from small heights. It is a mental state of all humans that they can scale only up to a particular height safely and this differs widely from person to person.

In addition, he approves designs of the safety system for safe working including falling of material on ground which may injure a person walking by. All over the world, one can see that the top few floors of a building, when under construction, are covered on the outside by galvanized iron sheets and safety nets spread all around the building.

State Government's labour commissioner and his managers also make periodical visits to all sites and have the authority to stop work if found unsafe to work in.

In case of accidents and deaths of workmen, government pays for treatment and compensation through employees' state insurance corporation (ESIC). In India, an act to this effect was enacted by the Indian parliament in 1948. ESIC charges a fixed sum from the company every month, worked out on the basis of the number of employees, their salary and the age of all employees and nature of the risks involved. As on date, in India, only workmen are covered under this scheme and have opened their own hospitals in many parts of the country. In the developed world, even the staff and directors are covered by medical insurance sponsored and monitored by the government.

Further, there is a misconception that expenditure on safety is a waste. The engineer has two alternatives.

Alternative 1

- Pay very heavy insurance premiums. Past performance and management of safety concerns are factors to decide insurance premium.

- Maintain a full-fledged dispensary at site or give a service contract to a private hospital.

- Damage to equipment and injuries to the workforce due to accidents.

- Pay a few workmen compensations with top-up Ex-Garcia payments in case of serious injuries.

- Loss of man hours.

Alternative 2

- Pay minimum insurance premium.

- Efficient and safe working.

- Minimal loss of man hours on the project.

Alternative 2 is always cheaper and is being enforced strictly all over the world including in developing countries.

Environment

Care of environment has now become a global concern and is now filtering down to common man, even in undeveloped countries. They plant a few trees before cutting a tree. The basic ideology is that your acts should not be deterrent to others and to society. Everybody understands that your work may be important but still, it can be done without or least hurting others.

Common environment-friendly acts are like:

- Not to smoke in the presence of non-smokers. They would have to perforce inhale the smoke released by you.

- Not to cut trees; they convert carbon dioxide into oxygen and give fruits and shelter from the sun.

- Use of proper toilets to avoid spreading of germs.

- Avoiding formation of water ponds which brew mosquitoes.

- Etc.,

On construction sites, one can further contribute to environment protection by doing the following:

- Sprinkle water on construction roads and work area as often as required to reduce dust formation.

- Properly cover trucks carrying loose earth or other construction material to avoid spilling over on roads and dust creation. A small piece of a pebble-like stone could smash the windscreen of a vehicle passing by at a high speed and cause accidents.

- Avoid cutting trees and plant more trees if cutting is unavoidable.

- Make proper and hygienic ways of sewage disposal.

- Keep the workplace and living camp clean and hygienic.

- Etc.

11.2 Planning and scheduling

On a project, the contractor is given a section of the project or the whole of the project to execute in a defined and agreed timeframe. He should first plan his work and then monitor his planning regularly, taking corrective steps as necessary. On large projects, a separate department headed by a planning engineer is created. They monitor the planning and progress of work of all section engineers and report it to the Project Manager with a consolidated report. This report is deliberated in progress reviews on a weekly or a fortnightly basis, which is also an evaluation process of performance of all the section engineers and sometimes, on repeated non-performance, adverse decisions are also taken.

Project planning should include the following:

1. Study the job briefly and find out the scope of work.

2. Go to the project site and see the physical condition.

3. If it is barren or has thick vegetation, understand the surface—see if it is level, dry, swampy or hilly.

4. Assess the surface; is it soft muddy, sandy or rocky. If it is rocky, which is type of rock, i.e., igneous, sedimentary or metamorphic.

5. Does it need blasting for digging foundations?

6. What are the logistic challenges like road connectivity distance from camp and office, local habitation, etc.?

7. Any other details you think or have been advised to explore.

8. Spend some time in the office on the documents, discussions with superiors how and when the job is to be executed.

9. Time available for the execution of a job including time required for mobilization of resources.

10. What are the resources available handy and the challenges to mobilize additional resources, i.e., workers, supervisors, engineers, technicians and equipment operators, construction materials, construction equipment, construction and working drawings, safety requirement, housing, market for daily needs drinking water and electricity and their reliability?

11. Is it mandatory to carry out some soil or other tests as per contract?

12. With this, most of the information is available and side by side it will be nice, if someone has worked out approximate quantities of work like earthwork, piling, concrete of a grade and type, reinforcement bars steel structures, embedment's, fittings and fixtures, etc., with their specifications.

13. Now, make a fair assessment of what and how work could be done with the available resources and how long it will take to get additional resources.

14. Here comes a little bit of innovative engineering to work out how safely, as per quality standards in the contract, fast and economically this project can be executed with maximum utilization of local materials, manpower, equipment and other resources.

15. Divide the whole time available into two sections: time to start first activity, what all could be done with available resources and sequence of start of activities. Balance to wait for new resources, possibility of overlapping different activities and time for commissioning and hand over.

16. Prepare the first draft note on the method of construction, also called construction methodology.

17. Prepare the project time schedule covering all the activities and time to be spent for each activity.

18. Work out the resources required for each activity and the duration of their requirement.

19. Draw a graph of quantity against time of major resources separately for each resource; generally, it would have many ups and downs. Now, you need to adjust the time for various activities for optimum utilization of all the resources, called balancing of the schedule.

20. Work out the cost of the resources needed to complete the project.

21. Final trimming of the method statement and time schedule is to be done and submitted for approval and plan execution as approved by superiors.

22. It is furthermore important to monitor the progress of work and costs. Compare actual with planning and carry out necessary changes and modifications as work progresses in the project schedule and resources as necessary.

23. Your planning should also not be too aggressive; moderately aggressive is always preferred, by keeping margins for delays in activities towards the end of the project.

24. Project team should not be kept on too much pressure to avoid fatigue.

12

Costing and Tendering

Costing is the forecast of the costs of a project till the completion. If the cost is not properly worked out at the time of tendering, losing the tender due to high price is preferred instead of getting the tender at a very low price.

Taking a job at a very low price is not only a loss to the organization, but also creates a lot of problems in cash flow management during execution. This causes delays which further increase the costs due to overstay in the project.

Most contractors take advance payment at the beginning of the job and provide bank credits to run the project at the cost of the project. Thus, it is very important that the project starts earning from the first month itself and planning and pricing has to be done accordingly. A good contractor should know the principle of "how to fry the fish with its own oil." If one puts fish on a frying pan and heats it slowly, the fish would release oil and keep on frying as oil keeps on releasing with the speed complemented by both activities. In the same way, project should be executed.

A construction project is generally divided into the following cost components

- Materials

- Equipment to be procured and installed in the project

- Construction equipment

- Temporary and ancillary works

- Safety

- Human resources

- Project management and supervision

- Overheads

- Insurances

- Finance costs

- Risks and their mitigation

- Head office overheads

- Any other costs

- Contingencies

- Profit before tax

12.1 Materials

Major materials in civil engineering projects are

- Cement

- Sand

- Stone chips

- Rock in different sizes

- Embankment fills

- Bitumen in different grades

- Steel reinforcement in different grades and sizes

- Structural steel and plates

- Timber

- Any other material required for project

- Building materials including electrical items, doors, windows, ironmongery, sanitary ware, plumbing and drainage material, air conditioning ducting, hardware and other items as required in the contract

- Any specific materials that may be required but are not included in above list.

Cost of each unit of quantity of materials at site would have following components

- Purchase price including delivery to site with taxes, etc.

- Any processing work to be included in costs

- Royalties, etc., payable

- Loading, transport and unloading at site

- Total unit cost—sum total of above unit costs

Quantities for execution of works are available before start of costing for each type of material, preferably worked down to monthly requirements. The engineer is advised to fill up the unit costs and monthly quantities in a table for each type of material to get total cost of material for each month of project duration.

12.2 Costs of equipment to be procured and installed in the project

This would have generally following cost components:

- Cost ex works including loading on truck/trailer at time of dispatch.

- Transport cost

- Unloading at site

- Transit insurance

- Inspection before dispatch and on arrival at site by an expert for any defects/damages

- Repairs if needed

- Assembly at site including cranes, etc., if needed

- Preparation of foundation including foundation bolts and nuts

- Vibration pads if needed

- Erection of equipment on foundation including fitments if any

- Erection and commissioning supervision by manufactures representative

- First fill of fuel and lubricants

- Commissioning

- Supply of mandatory spares and/or as desired by owner

- Safe storage of spares

- Operation of equipment in guarantee period as per terms of contract

- Handover formalities

12.3 Till final handover of expensive equipment, contractor's engineers should not take any responsibility for the equipment and all responsibilities should rest on insurance company and/or supplier's representative.

12.4 Similarly, costs for each component of project are calculated for each month of the project duration for other items in the above list. And by this process, the total price is arrived at.

13

Pricing a Contract

Price worked out as per clause 12.4 is an indicative price worked out by estimation team with certain margins and contingencies indicated in their statements. The client generally provides an indicative price of the contract in his tender document and final tender winning price is generally within 15% plus or minus of this number.

Before deciding the final price to quote, the contractor should look to the following considerations:

Is he mentally prepared to take this contract? The following contribute to his mental state:

1. Technical competency to execute the job

2. In-house resources available

3. Reputation of the client

4. Capital investment and floating capital needed

5. Risks and contingencies

6. Future prospects after doing this job

7. Extent of his personal or CEO's involvement needed and would it be available.

8. Return on investment including in-house resources

9. Does the expected profit attractive?

He can change the price by changing numbers mainly for items 5, 6, 7, 8 and 9.

Then, the contractor or his authorized representative decides whether to participate or not in the tender and at what price. This final price is known to only one or two persons.

Pricing the tender

According to the terms of the tender document, a successful contractor has to give various guaranties as detailed in clause of this book.

The client may also provide advances for mobilization of resources and construction equipment and these advances against guarantees may or may not be interest-bearing.

Overall, the contractor commits a lot to the client to safeguard the client's risks and interests at the very start of the project.

The contractor can reduce this burden by submitting prices in following manner.

Instead of taking advance against bank guarantee, price could be split in two parts.

In first part, introduce activities like the following in preliminaries as payments instead of advance.

- Mobilization of project manager at site

- Mobilization of key equipment at site

  o Excavators

  o Cranes

- o   Concrete batching plant
- o   Etc.,
- Establishment of project office
- Camp facilities
- Cost of supervision per month for contract period
- Site overheads like stores, accounts, security, office, etc.
- Etc.

Sum total of the above is about 30% of the contract value and the rest is distributed among items of bill of quantities, related to their costs.

Equipment installed on the project could be broken down in BOQ as costs for placing order, dispatch from factory, received at site, erection and commissioning.

14

Execution of the Contract

Before the contract is awarded and signed, the draft agreement should be thoroughly studied for any variations to general agreements and understanding.

Engineer-in-charge of the project should also read the contract before/after award for execution as per terms agreed. There are usually unnecessary expenses due to misappropriation/ignorance of the contract conditions.

Health, safety, quality and productivity are major concerns of any contractor.

Project time schedule should be monitored and any changes in methods of execution, sequence of execution or resources requirement should be promptly addressed and necessary actions must be taken.

Progress bills should be prepared correctly without any omission and regularly submitted with proper follow-up for quick/timely release of payments by the client.

Work quantities and material reconciliation should be done at least monthly.

Procurement of materials should be as per agreed/revised specifications and concurrent to progress of work.

15

Record Variations to the Contract

Important to maintain a project diary to be written on a daily basis, covering weather conditions, progress of work, additional works ordered/executed, any variations and stoppage of work due to any reason.

All major items of the day's progress should be submitted to client as a daily progress report.

All the matters which **may** affect time and cost of the project should be informed to client through a simple letter.

At periodical intervals, the client should be informed of requesting additional payments and time for reasons contained in the previous correspondence.

Claims for such additions should be precipitated and submitted in writing at comfortable intervals but before specified in contract. They should not be time-barred.